MW01034352

WHEN COFFEE AND KALE COMPETE

Become Great at Making Products People Will Buy

Second Edition

Alan Klement

TABLE OF CONTENTS

FOREWORD

by Rick Pedi and John Palmer

ORIGIN OF CUSTOMER JOBS THEORY

Back in the days of the quality management movement (mid 1980s), the foundational tenet was that customers define quality. And so, deploying the Voice of the Customer (the VOC) throughout work processes became the central theme for improving business performance. This was especially true in product development, where design teams obsessed about gathering the VOC. In concept, properly researching the VOC would keep developers on track – not over-investing in features customers did not value, and thus, lose money, while not under-investing in features customers did value, and thus, lose customers. It was from this quality management perspective and the high business hopes of deploying the VOC that we created Customer Job Theory (JTBD) - together with Bob Moesta, Pam Murtaugh, and Julia Wesson.

Because we are the original source of Customer Jobs, Alan Klement has reached out to us to share his JTBD thinking and to ask our point-of-view on the evolution of JTBD Theory in light of its actual foundational roots. With that in mind, he asked us to write this foreword for his book.

BEYOND PRODUCT ATTRIBUTE QUALITY AS VALUE

JTBD Theory represented a major shift in the focus of product developers and the kind of market research used to support product development. The thinking behind Customer Jobs was the hard-learned understanding that developers and marketers needed to adopt a new paradigm about the meaning of value-for-customers. Instead of attaching value to what products are, value should attach to what products do for customers. In other words, stop trying to communicate value with new and improved product features, and start designing more integrated product experiences that are valuable because of what they enable customers to get done in particular contexts of use.

Our thinking called for new market research techniques that got beyond the prevailing methods that had customers evaluating products and describing lifestyle personas. Instead, we grounded customer interviews in recent real-life

5

purchasing and use situations. We learned how customer behavior derives directly from how customers perceive their market-use situation. No one else can know their situations better than customers do. And we would disguise our research purposes to enable customers to tell us what they actually did and why they did it - openly, expressively, and with emotion.

Our early Jobs research work never failed to generate amazing gaps between the reasons producers believed customers purchased products in the category (e.g., products were healthy, indulgent, or more convenient) and actual Job purposes customers had for "hiring a product".

Business growth opportunities could be found in the degree to which the Job that heavy users were hiring the product category to do had not yet been discovered by light or non-users of the category. And optimizing the product design to do the Job better and then communicating the Job value became a good strategy for growing sales.

AN EARLY EXAMPLE

The early JTBD evangelists that we taught and inspired began using Snickers as the de facto standard-bearer for communicating the idea that customers hire products to do Jobs. Ever since 1930, consumers experienced the typical candy bar ingredients of chocolate and nougat combined with whole peanuts more as real food than a candy treat. And yet, it wasn't until 1979 - when Mars introduced the tag "Snickers really satisfies" – that Snickers reflected "new thinking". Much more than a quality cue, "packed with peanuts" gave customers a reason to connect Snickers use with every day hunger situations.

The Snickers example easily demonstrated several fundamentals of JTBD Theory that are now commonplace:

> There are often wide gaps between the value producers think customers assign to their products and the real reasons customers have for using the category.

> Marketing communications should focus on what a product does for (and to) the customer, not on what it is. A Snickers satisfies hunger – i.e., what it does. It is chocolate and nougat combined with whole peanuts.

How the design of products can be perfected against the customer's hiring criteria. The food-like qualities of peanuts, Snickers' first bite and chew characteristics, its shape, and its weight in the hand all combine to signal and deliver against the requirements of satisfying hunger in certain customer Job situations.

The pitfalls and limitations of defining markets and competition in terms of product categories, versus, seeing markets from the customer's perspective. Mars came to understand that Snickers and Milky Way, which were thought of as "candy bars, chocolate confections, etc." were actually hired by customers for very different reasons. The slogan "Milky Way, comfort in every bar" recognized the differences between customers hiring Milky Way to do a "comfort me" Job and the same customers hiring Snickers to do a "satisfy my hunger" Job.

JTBD THEORY AND INNOVATION SUCCESS

Over the last 15 years, we've continued to advance the thinking we pioneered with JTBD Theory. Our focus has gone beyond using Jobs to explain customer choices. Instead, we have advanced core JTBD principles in order to understand how to develop new product concepts able to carve out new growth footholds in established, fiercely-competitive markets.

We also have followed closely Clayton Christensen's popularization of JTBD Theory and the connections to innovation he and his followers have made. In paraphrasing Clay:

> A Job is the progress that an individual is trying to make in a particular circumstance. And for innovators, understanding the Job is to understand what customers care most about in that moment of trying to make progress … i.e., the causal mechanism of customer behavior. Therefore, JTBD Theory provides a way of understanding the foundational question of innovation success: what causes a customer to purchase and use a particular product or service.

We respectfully disagree with the assertion that answering that question is the key to innovation success (of course that depends on your definition of innovation). How can you expect to invent new value propositions that will create tomorrow's markets ... with an understanding of customer progress that only explains why customers buy products today?

Moreover, understanding what customers care most about in that moment of trying to make progress, brings us back to the very beginning - JTBD Theory as way for businesses to grow sales by improving performance against the customer's definition of quality – essentially aligning today's products and services with the real reasons customers are buying them.

Our work, on the other hand, has led to asking and answering a very different question as the foundational question of innovation success: how do individuals develop themselves by using the marketplace to advance towards the values, norms, and ideals that enrich the meaning of their lives. After all, innovation is relevant only if it creates or leads customers to substantial new meaning in how they lead their lives. And by focusing on creating new market behavior versus explaining current behavior, we shift the innovator's work from explaining historical choices based on what a product does and is ... to understanding why and how customers would develop new market knowledge and behavior tomorrow.

ALAN'S WORK AND WHAT'S NEXT

In light of our work, we find Alan's thinking to be a breath of fresh air. Through determination and perseverance, he has developed the forward-looking "Self-Betterment" concept to explain the demand side of innovation. He makes a compelling case for Self-Betterment as a basis for innovators to work out what should be next. His case stands in stark contrast to prevailing JTBD Theory that can only explain today's customer choices.

Alan's work recognizes that humans have a compelling imperative to improve themselves. His thinking echoes the work we have been doing to explain why people, whose needs are already well met, still hunt the market for new ideas.

In our view, the Self-Betterment idea is on track and Alan is poised to develop it further in this direction: Human beings don't stand still. And in living their lives, they are restless innovators who use their environment - in this case the ecosystem of market information - to imagine better scenarios to their status quo ... to change existing situations to preferred ones ... to imagine what ought to be next in living their lives.

Step-change business growth demands that new product concepts reflect the improvement imperative that keeps customers looking to the market for ideas, devices, and knowledge that break from the past. The "next book" should fill in a picture of work we are now doing with causal models that explain how customers actually use the market to transform themselves and lift their capabilities for living the lives they imagine.

ACKNOWLEDGMENTS

This book does not represent insights from one person, but from many. Those listed here—as well as those whose names I have mistakenly omitted—have helped me understand JTBD and thereby helped me write this book. I am indebted to them and the entire JTBD community.

Tim Zenderman, Samuel Hulick, Leslie Owensby, Michael Sacca, Willis Jackson III, Morgan Ranieri, Andrej Balaz, Daphne Lin, Matthew Woo, Matt Brooks, Mat Budelman, Eric White, David Wu, Bob Moesta, John Palmer, Rick Pedi, Chris Spiek, Ervin Fowlkes, Timur Kunayev, Matthew Gunson, Alex Yang, Ryan D. Hmesatch, Leslie Owensby, Marc Galbraith, Daryl Choy, James Ramsay, Joshua Porter, Tor L. Bollingmo, Martin Jordan, Ryan Singer, Laura Roeder, Justin Jackson, Vincent van der Lubbe, Ash Maurya, Benedict Evans, Esteban Mancuso, Des Traynor, Paul Adams, Sian Townsend, and the rest of the Intercom team, Daniel Ritzenthaler, Dan Martell, Anthony Francavilla, Omer Yariv, Justin Sinclair, Joanna Wiebe, Paulo Peres, Alexander Horré, Bleau Alexandru, Tom Masiero, Jose A. de Miguel, Dimitri Nassis, Roman Meliška, Paul Gonzalez, Lee Yanco, Thomas Fröhlich, Lou Franco, David Emmett, Thomas Huetter, Nir Benita, Kyle Fiedler and Trace Wax and the thoughtbot team, everyone at the NYC JTBD Meetup, Amrita Chandra, Jeremy Horn, David Lee, Barry Clark, Ryan Witt, Boris Grinkot, Alex Lumley, Claudio Perrone, Omar Gonzalez, Ain Tohvri, Amit Vemuri, Sri Vemuri, Hiten Shah, Paul Sullivan, Matthew Woo, Joanna Wiebe, George White, Dave Rothschild, Elvin Turner, Mike Rivera, Jason Evanish, Levi Kovacs, and Debbie Szumylo.

Alan Klement

October 2, 2016

1 Challenges, Hope, and Progress

Challenges
Hope
About me
How to be successful with JTBD and this book
Abandon every MBA, all you who enter

This book will help you become great at creating and selling products that people will buy. Your joy at work will grow. You will know how to help companies increase revenue, reduce waste, remain competitive, and make innovation more predictable and profitable. In doing so, you will help economies prosper and help provide stable jobs for employees and the families who depend on them.

I struggled with innovation for many years. I finally made progress when I focused on two things:

> The desire every customer has to improve themselves and their life-situations.

> How customers imagine their lives being better when they have the right solution.

This understanding has helped me become a better innovator. I believe it will do the same for you. Yet, challenges stand in your way. This chapter introduces these challenges. The rest of this book will equip you with the understanding of how your focus on the customer's desire for self-betterment as a Job to be Done (JTBD) will help you overcome these challenges.

CHALLENGES

Creative destruction is accelerating. The average time a company spends on the S&P 500 continues to drop. In 1960, it was fifty-five years; in 2015, it was about twenty (figure 1). This happened for numerous reasons. A big one is that it has never been easier to create a product and get it to customers. This increases the pace at which new innovations disrupt the sales of incumbent ones and then go on to replace them. This process is known as creative destruction.[1]

Figure 1. Creative destruction in action. The average company life span on the S&P 500 index has declined over time (rolling seven-year average).

When one innovation wins, another loses. Why? Because a day has only so many minutes, and a customer can use only one product at a time. For example, every day I used to get an espresso from a coffee shop down the street. Two months ago, I bought a Nespresso machine. Now I make my own espressos. The coffee shop has lost my business.

The theory of Customer Jobs and the idea that customers buy a product to complete a Job to be Done, help us understand all the creative destruction around us. Even though solutions and technologies come and go, the customer's desire for self-betterment is always there. This focus on everyone's desire for self-betterment is the key to successful, ongoing innovation and business.

"Sunk costs" keep us from creating new products. In 1975, a Kodak engineer invented the digital camera. What was the management's response? They shelved it. Management argued that Kodak "could" sell a digital camera, but why would they? They made billions of dollars selling photographic film. A digital camera would cannibalize their film sales. In the end, Kodak's management decided that the company would skip digital and focus on selling photographic film.[2]

In 2012, Kodak filed for bankruptcy. What happened? Customers no longer needed film for their cameras—they had switched to digital cameras. Kodak's downfall was due to management's unwillingness to adapt to a world with digital cameras—something they had invented forty years earlier.

Why did Alan buy the Snickers?

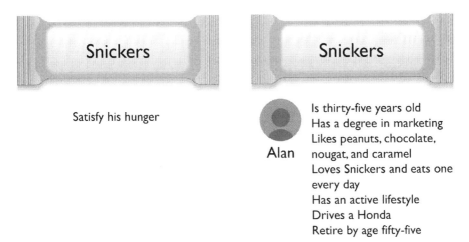

Snickers

Satisfy his hunger

Snickers

Alan

Is thirty-five years old
Has a degree in marketing
Likes peanuts, chocolate, nougat, and caramel
Loves Snickers and eats one every day
Has an active lifestyle
Drives a Honda
Retire by age fifty-five

Figure 2. What data about your product are information? Which are misinformation?

Very often, it's not legacy technology that stops companies from adapting, but being tied to a legacy business model. And when change is proposed to management, they have unlimited excuses to avoid it: "We make billions of dollars with our current products. Why risk it by selling something different?"; "We've spent a hundred years perfecting what we do and building the company we have today. Why should we change?" Excuses like these make it hard for businesses to adapt, but change will always happen. Customer Jobs gives you the confidence to break away from legacy business models and create the products of tomorrow.[3]

It's a mistake to focus on our customers' physical characteristics. My father-in-law is sixty-five years old, is from the Bronx, and has never used a computer in his life. I'm thirty-five years old, from Florida, and wrote my first computer program at fifteen. Our behaviors, physical characteristics, life goals, and personal histories couldn't be more different. Nevertheless, we both own the same model of smartphone. We even use it in almost the same way. Will a study of who we are and how we behave explain why? Which data in figure 2 are information? Which are misinformation?[4]

JTBD helps you become better at knowing the difference between good data and bad data. This helps you focus on making changes to your product that bring profits instead of increasing your costs of production only.

We don't take into consideration how customers see competition. In 2006, Indian manufacturer Godrej collaborated with Harvard Business School professor Dr. Clayton Christensen to create the chotuKool—a low-cost, feature-minimal refrigerator. It was hailed as a "disruptive innovation" that would create a new market of refrigerators and create what Christensen calls "inclusive growth" for millions of low-income Indians. Unfortunately, the chotuKool was a costly flop. What happened?

For far too long, academics and analysts—who have no personal experience with innovation—have created and sold pseudoscientific theories of innovation. Unfortunately, these theories often mislead. The resulting product failures exact terrible costs on our economies. This happens because most, and perhaps all, of these theories don't take into consideration how customers view competition. Do PCs compete with mainframes because they're both "computers," or do PCs compete with typewriters, video game systems, and accountants? Do hard drives compete only with other hard drives, or do they also compete with tape storage, CDs, DVDs, floppy disks, flash drives, and cloud storage?

JTBD helps you avoid mistakes like the chotuKool and falling victim to invalid theories of markets by giving you the knowledge to create an accurate model of competition before you create a product. It does this by helping you learn how to gain the customer's perspective on what does and doesn't count as competition for a JTBD.

We myopically study and improve on customers' "needs" and expectations of today; instead, we should create new systems that help customers make progress. In the 1860s, the Pony Express was created to help customers get letters and messages across the United States as fast as possible. It lasted only nineteen months. What happened? Western Union established the transcontinental telegraph. While the Pony Express was trying to solve the "needs" associated with using physical mail, Western Union thought, *what if we could communicate without using physical messages?* [5]

Very often, innovators think they are studying customers' needs – when in fact they are studying what customers don't like about the products they use today, or what customers currently expect from a product. For many years, manufacturers such as Nokia, Palm, Research in Motion (RIM), and Motorola worked hard to satisfy customers' stated needs and expectations: make a low-price smartphone with a physical keyboard. Today, those expectations have been reversed. Customers don't mind shelling out several hundred dollars for a smartphone, and physical keyboards have almost completely disappeared.

We can't build the products of tomorrow when we limit ourselves to the needs and expectations associated with the products of today. Instead, we should focus on what never changes for customers: their desire for progress. When we focus on delivering customers' progress—instead of what customers say they want—we are free to imagine a world where many needs and expectations are replaced with new ones. Customer Jobs theory helps us ask, "Customers keep asking for a smartphone with a keyboard, but couldn't we help customers so much more if we take it away?" Chapters 13 and 14 show you the power of prioritizing customer progress over everything else.

We may think about the upsides of product changes only, ignore the downsides, and fail to embrace new ways of helping customers make progress. In the early 1980s, the Coca-Cola Company was losing market share to Pepsi. In response, Coca-Cola's management decided to change the formula for Coke, believing that the change would increase market share. They were wrong. Loyal customers went up in arms over it; three months later, Coca-Cola's original formula was restored. Over time, the company regained its market share, but it was lucky. It had the money and resources to recover from the mistake.[6]

Customer Jobs helps you know when it does and doesn't make sense to change your product. Your product might be fine the way it is. Any further investment might increase only your costs of production. Customer Jobs also helps you understand the opportunity costs: what happens when you don't invest in new products, even if it means cannibalizing existing offerings? Kodak knows the cost of not embracing new ways of helping customers evolve: bankruptcy.

Our decision making can be misled when we manage by visible figures only. Customer Satisfaction Score (CSAT) and Net Promoter Score (NPS) are figures that seems straightforward enough. Ask customers to self-report their satisfaction with your product and record their responses. If CSAT or NPS are high, you're doing a good job. Easy, right? Yet, such data and figures are incomplete at best and misinformation at worst. In chapter 13, you'll learn about Spirit Airlines. Customers have consistently rated it as the worst airline in the United States. Nevertheless, it continues to be the fastest-growing and most profitable airline in America. If customers hate it so much, why do they keep flying it?

Figure 3. A tale of creative destruction. Chasing visible figures often leads to poor decisions about your product.

Figures can not only be misleading, they can also be misused. We see this today with the number of monthly active users (MAU) for Twitter. It has experienced explosive growth over the last five years—annual revenue was $106 million in 2011 and $2.2 billion in 2015. Yet analysts and journalists continue to write articles titled "The End of Twitter" and "A Eulogy for Twitter." Why?

The most common criticism is that growth of Twitter's MAUs has stalled at "only" 313 million. Is it any surprise when management's priority then becomes "How can we make MAUs go up?" instead of "How can we continue to make Twitter valuable to users, so they won't leave?" Yes, adding new features might push up visible figures such as MAU in the short term, but constant changes might upset and drive away loyal users. Instead, we should congratulate Twitter's employees for their hard work and gently remind them of grandmother's advice: "When you try and please everyone, you end up pleasing no one."[7]

Many innovators and managers have been influenced by ideas such as:

> If you can't measure it, you can't manage it.

> What gets measured gets improved.

However, such opinions do not take into consideration the following:[8]

> All models are wrong, but some are useful.

> The most important figures are unknown or unknowable, but successful management must nevertheless take account of them.

> If you torture the data long enough, they will tell you whatever you want.

> It is wrong to suppose that if you can't measure it, you can't manage it – a costly myth.

These statements were made by some of the most important mathematicians and systems thinkers of the twentieth century. They are warnings for those who subscribe to the idea of being driven by visible figures only, and not taking into consideration figures that are unknown or unknowable. Yes, visible figures can be helpful and are often necessary. We have payroll to meet and should strive to increase long-term profits. But we can let figure based data deceive us.

We must remember that data are only proxies for some results of a system. Moreover, the most important figures are unknown and unknowable. What figures or data would have told Apple to remove floppy drives from PCs or keyboards from their smartphones? At the time, many dismissed or criticized these ideas. Journalists claimed Apple's management had lost their minds. Now we regard Apple's decisions as obvious. And what about Twitter's MAUs? The number of users who might want a product like Twitter is a figure that is unknown and unknowable. Twitter's 313 million MAU might represent 100 percent of the market. Analysts, journalists, and even Twitter's own shareholders might be punishing the company even as it achieves market dominance.

There are a variety of consequences that arise when we abandon intuition and risk taking in favor of management by visible figures only. Perhaps the worst are the unfounded beliefs that a product will last forever, and that products and companies can continuously grow revenue and attract more customers. The reality is that growth for every product will slow and stop. Nothing lasts forever.

Unfortunately, many managers either don't know or won't accept this. Instead, they become worried when growth slows. They start making changes to their product in hopes of attracting more customers and increasing revenue;

however, the effect is often the opposite. Management ends up making the product worse for existing customers. With some luck, a competitor won't notice.[9]

But luck will eventually run out. Another innovation will enter the market with a product that customers find more valuable (figure 3). Why? Because the entrant's innovation cuts off all the baggage the incumbent added during management's frantic attempt to push up all those visible figures. This is when customers begin to switch from the incumbent to the newcomer. So, goes the cycle of creative destruction.

Innovation is hard, risky, and nerve-racking. Just ask anyone who has successfully done it. But Customer Jobs can help. With the correct point of view, we can see how visible figures tell us about individual parts of a system only. Once we understand that, we can apply Customer Jobs thinking and understand the relationships around the data. This gives us the ability to assign the proper weight to these figures—or even dismiss them. This helps us become better at knowing if we should continue to improve an existing product or take a risk and develop a new one.

HOPE

Customer Jobs theory and this book offer you hope whether you are a struggling innovator or just want to become better at understanding, marketing, innovation, product design, or all three. Customer Jobs gives you a collection of principles for understanding why customers buy and use products. This singular attention to customer's desire for self-betterment—instead of what customers say they want, their demographics, or what they do—is what distinguishes Customer Jobs from other theories. This book aims to explain the theory reliably and consistently.

At the time of this writing (2015), no comprehensive book about Customer Jobs theory exists. This is the first. Many others have written interpretations of some of its principles, but almost all of them have created more confusion than clarity.

This book stands out from other writings about Customer Jobs because its contributors—including me—are all innovators and entrepreneurs in our own right. We've applied the theory to our own businesses and products, rather than merely study and preach it.

I developed this book and Customer Jobs theory as if I were creating a product. For Customer Jobs to be successful, it must deliver progress to those who plan on using it. This is why I interviewed sixty-three innovators about their struggles with innovation and how Job to be Done helped them design a better product. I extracted numerous case studies and insights from these interviews. The most comprehensive and useful ones are featured in this book.

I had to combine my experiences with those of these innovators to design Customer Jobs into what it should be. I learned something from every practitioner I talked with. I am in their debt. Of course, you benefit the most. With this book, you add the accumulated experience of many successful innovators to your own. This collective knowledge will help you become better at creating and selling products that customers will buy.

THE PROGRESS YOU CAN MAKE WITH CUSTOMER JOBS

Customer Jobs is attractive to many because it offers you progress in many ways. Here are a few of my favorite.

Alignment and distributed decision-making. Insights around a customer's Jobs to be Done serves as a "true north". Everyone in the business will use the same customer insights to market, design, build, and manage solutions that customers will buy and use to make progress in their lives. This empowers employees throughout the organization to make good decisions that align with the job, be autonomous and innovative.

Know what data are and are not needed for innovation. Innovators created Customer Jobs theory for themselves. We didn't create it to sell books, collect speaking fees, sell MBA diplomas, or get a PhD from a business school. We created Customer Jobs because we needed help creating successful products that could support our families. In order to do this, we had to figure out what data were and were not relevant to our innovation efforts.

When we design, we're faced the countless trade-offs involved in developing a business strategy, crafting advertising, designing, and engineering, from which questions like these arise:

We can't attack every market. Which ones should we focus on?

Our video ad must connect with customers in just five seconds. How can we do that?

Which shade of white will help customers experience luxurious but not sterile?

Which alloy should the suspension be made of to give customers the "feel the road" experience?

Once you know that you need answers to questions like these, you know which data are and are not important. Not only that, you know what should and should not be measured – as well as what can and cannot be measured.

Not everything that can be counted counts, and not everything that counts can be counted.

—William Bruce Cameron

JTBD helps create and sustain a growth culture: What happens when you don't have a healthy growth mindset? You end up wasting time and money building products and features that don't increase revenue. I learned that lesson the hard way – both when I was a Product Manager and as an entrepreneur.

JTBD immunes us with the idea that organizations grow when they offer a growth opportunity to existing and potential customers. No one wants to solve their problems only, we want someone to also give us new and better ways to improve our life-situations in meaningful ways. This thinking helps us answer important growth-related questions such as:

How can we make sure people continue to buy our existing product?

How can we get more people to buy our product, or get them to buy more of it?

What additional products and services can we create that existing customers will also buy?

What additional products and services can we create that can gain us new customers.

Customer Jobs and its focus on progress gives us a way to think about and answer these questions.

Customer Jobs is a theory evolved over time. The principles of Customer Jobs draw on studies in statistical theory, economics, systems thinking, and psychology. Its principles have slowly evolved over time—at least seventy-five years. It is by no means a flavor of the month.

As a theory, Customer Jobs persists because it is completely decoupled from describing what kind of product you should make. Instead, it is purely focused on understanding how all customers desire to evolve themselves. You need such a theory to help you become better at innovation.

HOW TO BE SUCCESSFUL WITH CUSTOMER JOBS AND THIS BOOK

> As to methods there may be a million and then some, but principles are few. The man who grasps principles can successfully select his own methods. The man who tries methods, ignoring principles, is sure to have trouble.
>
> —Harrington Emerson

I don't believe there is any one "right" way to innovate. Life has too many unknown and unknowable variables. Successful entrepreneur Steve Blank illustrates this by saying, "No business plan survives first contact with a customer."[10]

Customer Jobs prepares us for whatever curveballs are thrown at us because it equips us with principles instead of methods. Why? Methods come and go, whereas principles stick around. In fact, when you're armed with the right principles, you can plug in any appropriate methods and mental models. You might even create your own methods. And while this idea may cause you some anxiety, over time you will find it empowering. The study and application of principles, instead of methods, is what gives you the confidence to act in a complex world.

While it's easier to teach and learn methods, you become a better designer and innovator when you ground yourself with principles. This is why this book focuses on principles and demonstrates those principles in action through case studies. Most chapters also have a "Put it to work" section that gives ideas on how to apply these principles.

About Me

I recommend Customer Jobs because I've applied its principles as an entrepreneur, product manager, designer, engineer, and salesperson. I've applied it to my own businesses and on products whose success I was directly responsible for. I believe it's wrong to preach a theory unless you've applied it yourself and were exposed to the risks in the event the theory failed.

Customer Jobs has helped me. I struggled with innovation for many years. I started my first business in 2003. It offered photographic services, image retouching, and a software platform where customers could create their own websites to showcase their artwork. It was a success. At the time, I didn't understand why it was successful. But now I do. It was because I offered a collection of products that worked together—as a system—to help customers make progress. What progress did those customers want? "Help me get recognition for myself and my work."

As my business grew, I saw myself transition from maker to manager. I didn't like it. So, I sold the business and went back to making things. I started another business called Vizipres. It failed. Why? I made a product that people would use, but not pay for.

I thought that perhaps I needed to learn from other entrepreneurs. I began working for others as an engineer and designer. Later, I began leading innovation efforts at various companies. Inspired by all this knowledge, I began a third business called AIM. After a few iterations, it ended up as an advertising marketplace for mortgage brokers and real estate agents. As soon as it gained momentum, I sold it to my cofounder. I learned long ago that I'm a maker, not a manager.

That's also when I realized that Customer Jobs, at the time, was incomplete. Many of the principles and suggested theory of the time were inconsistent and often contradictory. I decided to unpack, refine, and expand its principles to help others and myself.

And as of today – as I update the 2nd edition of this book – I'm in the process of applying JTBD theory to create another product. Keep an eye out.

ABANDON EVERY MBA, ALL YOU WHO ENTER

I invite you to explore JTBD with me. I also ask that you—at least for the time being—put aside any preconceived notions of competition, markets, and even Customer Jobs. You can pick them up again when the book is finished, or you may decide you no longer need them.

PART I

The Job to be Done

Our journey begins with an introduction to Customer Jobs theory and the idea of a customer having a Job to be Done (JTBD). This section will equip you with a strong foundation to understand what it means to study Customer Jobs and why it is a vital part of innovation.

2 WHAT IS A JOB TO BE DONE (JTBD)?

My JTBD creates a new me
What isn't a Job to be Done?
A Job to be Done defined
Products enable customers to get a Job Done
Where does Customer Jobs theory come from?

> Upgrade your user, not your product. Don't build better cameras—build better photographers.
>
> —Kathy Sierra

Ten thousand years ago, we were hunter gatherers and used our feet to roam the earth. Today, we have fast food restaurants and autonomous cars. Why did we change? Because we have an intrinsic desire to transform our life-situations into something better. We do this by remaking and adapting to the world around us.

The desire to improve ourselves and our life-situations is in our DNA. It's what makes us human. Moreover, we do these transformations with purpose. We purposefully use the arts to improve ourselves emotionally; the sciences to improve ourselves intellectually; and engineering to improve how we interact with the world. Purposeful transformation is why we are different from animals:

> A bear trying to catch food by the river may think: I wish fishing could be made better, faster, or easier.

> But only a human will think: Fishing is no good. If I could transform that lagoon over there into a place where I can breed fish, then I'd never have to go fishing again.

The bear thinks only about what is. Today, it may come up with a better, faster, or easier way to fish. But tomorrow, it is still a bear that fishes. The human, on the other hand, thinks about what ought to be. Today, she fishes, but tomorrow that can change. If she could figure out a way to no longer do the fishing herself, then she can focus on improving other life-situations—like building a hut so she could move out of that dank cave.

29

The bear does not think about transforming itself or its world. It never has a Job to be Done. The human, on the other hand, can desire change. And every time she begins the process of transforming her life-situation, she has a Job to be Done.

IMPROVE YOUR LIFE-SITUATION; BECOME MORE THAN YOU ARE

Why are you reading this book? I guarantee you're not reading it for the sake of reading it only. Do you have any social or functional goals you aim to achieve? I doubt it. I'm not sure how a book can be described in terms of "functional" unless you use it as a door-stop. And social? Well, unless your plan is to tell everyone you've "read the most amazing book!" (a course of action I highly recommend), I don't see how there's any social element to it either. Besides, isn't every social action really a personal, emotional desire to gain recognition?

I don't think there are any social or functional purposes for reading this book. Rather, I believe you are reading this book because you hope to become better at creating and selling products that people will buy and use. And this Job to be Done of yours – make you better at making and selling products that people will buy – is why you are hiring this book. In fact, I bet you don't even want to read this book. You do so because it is the only way for you to gain the knowledge contained herein. If it were possible to download the knowledge into your brain – like the character Neo from the Matrix – you would probably choose that instead.

Job theory starts with the premise that we, as humans, always want to improve our various life-situations in a variety of ways. This exploration of our core desire to improve ourselves has a long philosophical tradition. The ancient Greek poet Pindar wrote about "becoming who you are". That is, the exploration and realization of the self is ongoing. This tradition has continued through recent times. The work of philosopher-psychologist Friedrich Nietzsche's advocates the humans-seek-self-betterment in various ways. Even Sigmund Freud picked up on this, offering the idea that we attach things to ourselves to become "prosthetic Gods."[11]

> It can be shown that every living thing does everything it can not to preserve itself, but to become more.
>
> —The Will to Power, Friedrich Nietzsche

Figure 4. What is Revlon really selling?

Now, I doubt you picked up this book to learn philosophy. My aim is to illustrate the idea that self-betterment is a core human desire. We should take advantage of this truth and use it in our efforts to create sustainable growth for our businesses. And interestingly, I don't think I'm the first one to have this idea.

Charles Revson, founder of Revlon, perfectly encapsulates a JTBD when he said:[12]

> In the factory, we make cosmetics. In the drugstore, we sell hope.

With these words, Revson marks the difference between what customers buy, and why they buy it. This thinking was also carried over into Revlon's advertising. In 1952, Revlon's breakout advertising campaign was Fire and Ice (figure 4). The advertising campaign makes it clear: Revlon isn't selling a product, it's selling transformation – the idea that, with this product in your life, you'll be able to create a "new me" that is desirable in ways your "existing me" is not. This idea of selling transformation is why there's barely any mention of any product in the ad. One whole page is a check list of provocative questions; the other features a picture of model Dorian Leigh. Only on further investigation do you notice the lipstick and nail polish at the bottom of the page.

A Job to be Done is neither found nor spontaneously created. Rather, it is designed. The checklist of provocative questions such as, "Have you ever wanted to wear an ankle bracelet?" exists to help customers imagine (i.e., design) what the new me will look and be like when they buy Revlon's products. Then there's the picture of Dorian Leigh. Upon seeing that, consumers continue to design a new version of themselves in their mind. For some, the new me looks like her. For others, the new me is with her. Whatever the case, if this new me who experiences new life-situations is something I want, I begin desiring it. In other words, I have a Job to be Done.

A JOB TO BE DONE DEFINED

Customer Jobs theory states that markets grow and transform whenever customers have a Job to be Done, and then buy a product to complete it (get the Job Done). This makes a Job to be Done a transformation process: it starts, it runs, and it ends. The key difference, however, is that a JTBD describes how a customer changes or wishes to change. We define a JTBD as follows:

> A Job to be Done is the process a consumer goes through whenever she aims to transform her existing life-situation into a preferred one, but cannot because there are constraints that stop her.

PRODUCTS ENABLE CUSTOMERS TO GET A JOB DONE

Humans are limited in our abilities. We can't change a life-situation by ourselves. A snap of our fingers cannot create a world where a morning commute is an enjoyable experience. Realizing such a change requires innovation on the part of oneself or someone else. Progress can only happen when we attach and integrate new ideas and new products into our lives.

An example of constructing (i.e., designing) a Job to be Done comes from a research project I led to understand what Job or Jobs customers were hoping to get Done (i.e., what new me customers were hoping to create) with a project management software. Here is a synopsis of one interview. Notice how the

This is most important to customers...   ...not this.

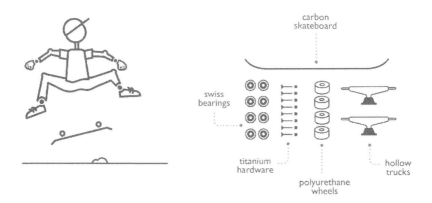

Figure 5. The designers at intercom (intercom.com) use this illustration to show the difference between what customers buy, and what they want.

hero of our story comes to realize a new me is possible, and how he must attach a product to himself to attain that new me:

> Andreas began a business around medical tourism. Over time, he grew his business to include five employees. One day, he was out with a friend of his, Jamie, at a coffee shop. During their conversation, Jamie mentioned a product called Basecamp to Andreas. Andreas had never heard of it. He was curious to learn more.
>
> Jamie explained to Andreas that Basecamp was a project management tool that helped small businesses become better at organizing themselves. Andreas was surprised by this. He knew about complicated project management products like Microsoft Project, but those were for big companies only, not smaller ones like his. Currently, Andreas was using Google Sheets, Google Docs, and e-mail to run his company. He just assumed that, well, that's how companies his size operated.
>
> Jamie further explained that Basecamp was made specifically to help companies his size. As Jamie spoke, Andreas's mind began racing: Basecamp could help my company stay organized as it adds more customers and employees. Up until this point, he had just assumed that his company had hit its growth limit.

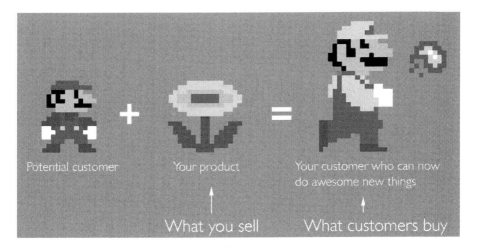

Figure 6. Samuel Hulick uses this illustration to show how customers use products to design a "new me".

Andreas and Jamie enjoyed their coffee and parted ways. During his train ride home, Andreas looked up Basecamp on his mobile device. He also learned about and investigated similar products to Basecamp. In the end, he decided to go with Basecamp. He signed up or it, began using it, and grew his company beyond five employees for the first time.

This is what a Job to be Done looks like. A consumer goes along his life as he's come to know it. Then things change. He is presented with an opportunity to improve his life-situation—in this case, make changes so he can grow. When or if he finds a product that helps him realize that growth opportunity, he can evolve to that better version of himself he had imagined. In the case of Andreas, Basecamp enabled him to gain control over how his business could be run. This enabled him to grow it beyond a few employees for the first time.

Besides demonstrating a JTBD well, Andreas's story also demonstrates that creating a new me (i.e., having a JTBD) is a process. It's not something that consumers have; it's something consumers participate in. That's why it's called a Job to be Done. A comparable example is falling in love. Falling in love isn't something you have; it's something you participate in. And just as you can't complete the fall-in-love process by yourself, a customer can't complete a JTBD by himself. He needs a product to help him design, construct, and complete it.

Customers are always beautifully, wonderfully dissatisfied, even when they report being happy and business is great. Even when they don't yet know it, customers want something better, and your desire to delight customers will drive you to invent on their behalf.

No customer ever asked Amazon to create the Prime membership program, but it sure turns out they wanted it, and I could give you many such examples.

—Jeff Bezos[13]

WHAT ISN'T A JOB TO BE DONE

While many of us have been applying Customer Jobs for a while—Rick Pedi and John Palmer have been developing Customer Jobs since the 1990s—it has gained popularity only recently. And like so many things that spread quickly, many people have distorted and misinterpreted it.

The biggest mistake I see is thinking of a Job to be Done as an activity or task. Examples include store and retrieve music, listen to music, cut a straight line, or make a quarter-inch hole. These are not Jobs; rather, they are tasks and activities – which means they describe how you use a product or what you do with it. For example, music streaming products such as Pandora and Spotify were designed specifically so customers didn't have to store and retrieve music like when they used CDs or MP3s. As far as listen to music, that is a broad activity that varies wildly depending on the context. Someone listening to music, so he can maintain his motivation during a workout is engaging in a very different activity than someone going to the opera to listen to music.

The problem with describing customer demand as activities is well articulate by the creator of Activity-Centered Design, Don Norman:[14]

> Harvard professor Theodore Levitt once pointed out, "People don't want to buy a quarter-inch drill. They want a quarter-inch hole!" Levitt's example of the drill implying that the goal is really a hole is only partially correct, however. When people go to a store to buy a drill, that is not their real goal. But why would anyone want a quarter-inch hole? Clearly that is an intermediate

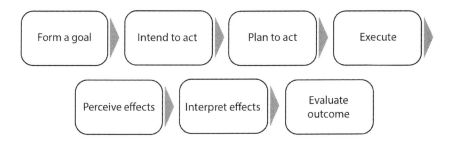

Figure 7. Don Norman's 1988 book, the design of everyday things, features activity-centered design and the seven stages of action seen here. This theory formed the basis of ideologies such as task analysis and human-computer interaction.

goal. Perhaps they wanted to hang shelves on the wall. Levitt stopped too soon.

Once you realize that they don't really want the drill, you realize that perhaps they don't really want the hole, either: they want to install their bookshelves. Why not develop methods that don't require holes? Or perhaps books that don't require bookshelves. (Yes, I know: electronic books, e-books.)

Besides, there are already brilliant design methods out there to help you design for tasks and activities. Examples include Activity Theory, Don Norman's Activity-Centered Design (figure 7), Cognitive Task Analysis, Goal Directed Design, Use Cases, and Human-Computer Interaction (HCI). If you want to learn more about how to design for activities or tasks, go there.

There are not different types of Jobs. Another common mistake is to think that there are types of Jobs. In particular, some may think there are emotional, function, and social Jobs. I'll describe why it's a bad idea from both a practical and theoretical perspective.

Practically, you'll be more successful when you think of every Customer Job as unique. We've learned that while many Jobs share the same core emotional desires (e.g., belonging, self-expression, control, etc.), each Job is a unique combination of these desires. That is why each product should deliver on these core emotional desires in its own way. A good example is Facebook. A lot of people use Facebook because it taps into desires such as control, self-expression, and belonging—but it does so in its own unique way. So instead of saying that

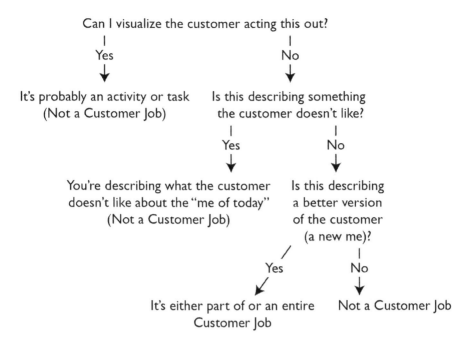

Figure 8. Are you describing a job to be done, or something else?

there are types of Jobs, you'll be much better off thinking that each Job is unique.

Theoretically—that is, from an ontological and epistemological perspective—Customer Jobs are design (artificial) problems, not natural problems. Natural problems are falsifiable. This means they can be objectively measured and determined as either true or false:

Q: Is argon (Ar) a noble gas?

A: If under conditions X it reacts, then yes; otherwise, no.

Design problems, on the other hand, are not falsifiable and cannot be measured objectively:

Q: How do we reduce crime?

Person 1: "Improve education."

Person 2: "Hire more police officers."

37

With respect to Jobs, then, no objective test can be created to say, "This is a social Job. That is not a social Job." If I buy a Ferrari to impress other people, is it a "social" Job because I want to impress other people? Or should we rephrase it as an insecurity, making it a "personal" or "emotional" Job?

And because there's no way to objectively define each type of Job, every person on the team will have his or her own opinion of what type of Job it should be. Moreover, even if/when you do get consensus, so what? Isn't knowing that I bought a Ferrari because I want to "fit in" good enough? What do you gain by labeling it a social or personal Job? I'll tell you: absolutely nothing.

Take it from me, don't waste your time trying to dissect Jobs into different types. It's about as productive as trying to answer, "How many angels can dance on the head of a pin?"

Is it a Customer Job? Does it describe an improved life-situation or something else? When presented with a possible description of a Customer Job, the best framework of thinking I can offer you is the decision tree in figure 8.

Keep in mind that a Job to be Done describes the "better me." It answers the question, "How are you better since you started using [product]?"and "Now that you have this product, what can you do now that you couldn't do before?" Renowned psychologist Albert Bandura described humans as "proactive, aspiring organisms". Customer Jobs carries this idea into markets, making the claim that we buy and use things to improve ourselves, to make progress. If you're not describing a Customer Job in terms of progress, you're probably describing something else.

WHERE DOES CUSTOMER JOBS THEORY COME FROM?

The greatest—and most helpful—theories are not created by one person but are the result of many people over a long period (figure 9). This is certainly the case with JTBD. Its principles have emerged from the work of a long lineage of researchers and innovators. Here are the most notable.

Joseph Schumpeter and creative destruction. The roots of JTBD thinking go back at least seventy-five years to Joseph Schumpeter and his introduction of creative destruction. Schumpeter observed that new innovations steal customers from incumbent offerings and then eventually go on to replace them.

Influencers	Customer Jobs Theory
Joseph Schumpeter Creative Destruction	New innovations displace incumbent ones
	Customers use only one solution at a time for a JTBD
	Competition can come from anywhere
Russell L. Ackoff, W. Edwards Deming System of Profound Knowledge	Study of interdependence and interactions
	Understanding customer motivation through synthesis
	Innovation should never stop
	Special case vs. normal variation
	Correlation is not causation
George Loewenstein	Anxieties of choice and action
Ann Graybiel	Customers fall back on their habits
Amos Tversky, Daniel Kahneman Cumulative Prospect Theory	Preference is context dependent
	Customers overvalue losses and undervalue gains
	Customers have a limit on what they value
Gary Klein Naturalistic Decision Making	Mental simulation of making progress with a product
	Customers have a "Job" they want "Done"
John Palmer, Rick Pedi, Bob Moesta Pam Murtaugh, Julia Wesson	Customers don't want the product; they want help making their lives better
& the JTBD community	Customers want progress

Figure 9. Influences of Jobs to be Done.

At one time, horses and ships were our primary methods of personal transportation. Eventually, trains replaced horses, but then cars and airplanes replaced those trains and ships.

Customer Jobs incorporates Schumpeter's insights as it seeks to understand why customers pick one way of doing things over another. Yes, innovators create new solutions, but the wheels of creative destruction turn only through the interaction between customers and innovators.

Customer Jobs also incorporates another one of Schumpeter's brilliant insights that is almost always overlooked. Schumpeter argued that competition should not be measured only among products of the same "type." He insisted that competition can come from anywhere. You might think you're alone in a market or have market superiority, but some competitor unknown to you could be stealing away your customers. Your only sign that something is wrong is decreasing sales. In chapter 8, we take a close look at Customer Jobs, creative destruction, and competition

W. Edwards Deming and systems thinking. Schumpeter's influence on Customer Jobs is restricted mostly to factors of market dynamics and competition; however, W. Edwards Deming has influenced Customer Jobs the most. Those who are familiar with his nearly sixty years of contribution to theories of management and innovation will recognize his fingerprints throughout this book.

Deming's most notable influence comes from his development of systems thinking, which I discuss in chapter 13. Throughout Deming's career, he frequently reminded businesses that producers and customers are connected by systems:

> The customer and producer must work together as a system.

> The consumer is the most important part of the production line.

Deming often challenged companies to remember creative destruction. He impressed on business leadership that simply making a product better and better—improving what already exists—wasn't enough. Sooner or later, someone will invent something new. He would tell businesses the following:

> Makers of vacuum tubes improved year by year the power of vacuum tubes. Customers were happy. But then transistor radios came along. Happy customers of vacuum tubes deserted vacuum tubes and ran for the pocket radio.

> A dissatisfied customer does not complain; he just switches.

Deming understood that improving products of today continually isn't enough: "We must keep asking, what new product or service would help our customers more? What will we be making five years from now? Ten years from now?" For Deming, the process of innovation should never stop.[15]

Psychology. On the psychology front, you'll run into influences from Gary Klein, Amos Tversky, Daniel Kahneman, George Loewenstein, and Ann Graybiel. These are psychologists and scientists whose work forms the foundations of behavioral economics and naturalistic decision making (NDM). Their work helps us understand how and why customers don't make rational decisions when buying and using products, are inconsistent in their opinions of products, and don't always act in their best interest. Customer Jobs understands that if you want to make a great product and to develop a message that connects with customers, you have to understand the emotional forces that shape their motivation.

Bringing it all together. Then, you arrive at John B. Palmer, Rick Pedi, Bob Moesta, Julia Wesson, and Pam Murtaugh. In the 1990s, they began working together to combine their respective experiences into the first Customer Jobs principles. They are the ones who came up with the idea and language that customers have "Jobs" that they are trying to get "Done."

Then, you get to me and this book. John, Rick, and Bob have personally influenced me more than I could ever express. Last but certainly not least, the entire JTBD community has had a tremendous influence on me. Without their application of and experience with JTBD, this book would not have been possible.

3 WHAT ARE THE PRINCIPLES OF CUSTOMER JOBS?

Here are a few JTBD principles that you will see demonstrated repeatedly throughout this book. There are others, but the principles below are perhaps the most useful and commonly used in the Customer Jobs community.

PRINCIPLES OF CUSTOMER JOBS

Customers don't want your product or what it does; they want help making themselves better (i.e., they want to transform a life-situation, make progress). Charles Revson knew that customers didn't want cosmetics, which are just colored oils. He also knew that customers didn't want what those cosmetics do, which is simply coloring skin. He understood that his customers wanted hope. This understanding of customer motivation has helped keep Revlon in business for eighty-four years. In 2015, its revenue topped $1.9 billion. It seems that selling hope is a profitable business.[16]

Focusing on the product itself, what it does, or how customers use it closes your mind to innovation opportunities. For example, if you sold drills, you might be tempted to think that people buy drills and bits because they want holes. But then 3M comes along and develops an entire line of damage-free hanging products that are designed specifically to eliminate the need for a drill or for making any holes. Another manufacturer, Erard, also avoided the "customers want holes" trap. It promotes a collection of TV mounts with a simple description: "The first TV wall-mount bracket with no drilling of the wall required." While you were convinced customers wanted holes, your competitors understood that customers wanted help improving their lives.[17]

People have Jobs; things don't. It doesn't make sense to ask, "What Job is your product doing?" or say, "The Job of the phone is…" or "The Job of the watch is…" Phones, watches, and dry-cleaning services don't have Jobs. They are examples of solutions for Job.

Products don't have lives to make better. They also don't have motivations, aspirations, or struggles. However, people do struggle. They do have lives they want to improve. This is why people—not products—have a JTBD.

Competition is defined in the minds of customers, and they use progress as their criterion. Imagine an entrepreneur who wants to be advised and inspired by someone whom she respects. She has a variety of options to choose from to achieve this. Examples include reading books, watching videos, attending conferences, or giving advisory shares in exchange for mentorship.

The struggling entrepreneur cares little about how she gets advised and inspired. The concern is about making progress. "Are things better for me today than yesterday? Am I getting closer to that picture in my mind of how I want my life to be?" These are some of the criteria customers use to judge which products compete against one another to improve themselves. Customers don't define or restrict competition based on the functionality or physical appearance of a product. Instead, they use whatever helps them make progress against a JTBD.

When customers start using a solution for a JTBD, they stop using something else. Many solo entrepreneurs struggle with feelings of isolation and hope to be motivated and inspired. To get this Job Done, some choose to create local get-togethers through Meetup.com and encourage other solo entrepreneurs to join. If that doesn't work, they may try getting people together in an online chat group. If that doesn't work, they may decide to join an existing online community, such as Product People Club. If Product People Club, as a product, is something that works to make their lives better, they stop searching for new solutions. Their Job is Done.

These entrepreneurs were jumping from one solution to another. This makes competition for a JTBD a zero-sum game. For somebody to win, somebody else has got to lose. Just as only one puzzle piece can fit into an empty slot, a customer prefers only one solution at a time for a JTBD.

Innovation opportunities exist when customers exhibit compensatory behaviors. Baking soda was originally advertised as a baking agent. Over time, customers started using it as a cleaner and deodorizer. Arm & Hammer picked up on this. It now sells a variety of baking soda–based products specialized for various cleaning and deodorizing purposes.[18]

The Segway was meant to revolutionize personal transportation for the masses. It failed; however, it did find success among members of law enforcement who began using it for their patrols. Tour companies also began using Segways as the ultimate gimmick to attract tourists and for family activities.[19]

Baking soda and the Segway are examples of customers using products in ways for which they weren't originally intended. Such situations represent opportunities to innovate a new product or to refit an existing one.

Favor progress over outcomes and goals. Customer goals and outcomes are only the results of an action. The ball went into the net; that is a goal. Did you win the game? Are you becoming better at making goals? No one knows.

Measure progress instead. Making a goal today isn't as important as becoming better at making goals in the future. This philosophy is the same for your customers. They don't wait until after they've finished using a product to determine whether they like it. They measure progress along the way. Do people wait until they lose ten pounds before judging whether a gym membership is successful?

Customers need to feel successful at every touch point between themselves and your business, not just at the very end when the outcome of an action is realized. Design your product to deliver customers an ongoing feeling of progress. Over time, you will notice that you need to change the outcomes and goals you deliver to customers. Why? A successful product and business will continually improve customers' lives. As customers use your product to make their lives better, they will face new challenges and desire new goals and outcomes.

Progress defines value; contrast reveals value. See how easily you can answer this question: "Which food do you most prefer: steak or pizza?" Many people find this difficult to answer. An easier question might be, "When do you prefer steak, and when do you prefer pizza?"[20]

A customer may find it difficult to compare two foods without any context. The last question is easier because the person being asked is thinking about food and context together.

Products have no value in and of themselves. They have value only when customers use them to make progress. The value of steak is easier to assess when it's matched with a fancy restaurant and a nice bottle of wine. But things can get wacky in that scenario if we swap a slice of pizza for the steak.

The same effect, of course, also applies to pizza. A pizza birthday party for an eight-year-old makes perfect sense, but a steak birthday party for kids doesn't seem quite right. The kids would probably be upset and the party a disaster.

The same steak has more value at the fancy restaurant than at a kid's birthday party. The steak doesn't change, but its value does. Why? A steak at a fancy restaurant helps you have a better restaurant experience. It delivers progress. A steak at a child's birthday party does not make the party better. It does not deliver progress.

This is why we say progress defines value, and contrast reveals it. You understand the value customers place on a product when you compare and contrast the progress it delivers against the progress other products can deliver. A steak makes a fancy dinner better but a kid's birthday party worse. A pizza makes a fancy dinner worse but a kid's birthday party better.

Solutions for Jobs deliver value beyond the moment of use. Imagine you own a car. When it's sitting in your garage, is it still delivering value? Doesn't the satisfaction of owning a car extend beyond when you're actively using it? What's more valuable: getting transported from point A to point B or having the peace of mind that you have the ability to go where you want to go, whenever you like?

Our lives are dynamic. They can't be measured well in static terms. Yes, a solution can provide functionality only in the moment, but its value to the customer is realized in contexts beyond that moment. A product should be designed with an understanding of how it improves customers' lives, not just how it offers value in the moment.

Producers, consumers, solutions, and Jobs should be thought of as parts of a system that work together to evolve markets. What is a system? A system is a collection of parts that work together to achieve a desired effect. The value is not in any one particular part of the system but in how those parts work together.

A car is an example of a system. Imagine I give you a box that contains all the parts of a car. What I gave you would likely be worthless to you. The parts are valuable to you only when they are assembled in a particular fashion, when they work together in a particular way, and when you can use them to make progress. You become better at helping customers, not by studying the individual parts of the car, but by studying how those parts work together to create something that helps customers make progress.

The same is true for producers, consumers, solutions, and Consumer Jobs. You need to understand how these parts work together to evolve customers and renew markets. Such a study will also help you understand why and how customers and markets don't evolve.

Grill manufacturer Weber understands the idea of producers, consumers, products, and Jobs as part of a system. Weber understands that it's not in the business of making and selling grills. It's in the business of making people better grillers. That's why it offers educational materials, recipes, party-planning guides, grilling accessories, and even a free phone hotline for grilling advice. For many grillers, the JTBD is also about entertaining friends and family with cooking theater, as well as tasty food. In this case, it's about becoming a better host and entertainer. Weber understands that no matter how well its grills function, if customers can't use them to make progress against their JTBD, the grills are worthless.

The understanding that customers are buying a better version of themselves is why Weber delivers a constellation of products that work together—as parts of a system—to evolve consumers and markets. Weber has been a successful, profitable company since 1893.

 Use these to create a mental catalog of examples of what it is like to apply Customer Jobs to innovation efforts. This will help you absorb the concepts in this book and become better at applying the theory to your own innovation efforts.

After these case studies, we'll dig deeper into the forces that shape customer demand, why Customer Jobs practitioners claim that Jobs remain while solutions come and go, and what it is like when an innovation effort fails to account for the forces of progress and how customers see competition.

PART II

Demand and Competition

Customer Jobs theory encourages you to understand how demand for a product is generated and how customers view competition. The first three chapters in this part feature case studies of innovators who developed this understanding, and how it helped them create and sell products.

4 CASE STUDY: DAN AND CLARITY

What's the JTBD?
Put it to work

I didn't know who Dan Martell was when I started writing this book. Another Customer Jobs practitioner told me about Dan's success as a serial entrepreneur, angel investor, and Customer Jobs practitioner. When I did catch up with him, I learned that he had applied Customer Jobs principles while building a company called Clarity. Customer Jobs thinking helped him:

Improve his research efforts.

Understand the company's profit potential.

Understand how Clarity could stand out to customers.

Find marketing messages that resonate with customers.

Know which features his team should—and shouldn't—add to his product so that more customers would use it.

Founded in 2012, Clarity is a marketplace that connects entrepreneurs with experts who can advise, motivate, and inspire. Dan created Clarity to ensure that entrepreneurs get the advice they need to grow their businesses. It helps them find the right experts and then schedules and hosts calls with them. (Three years later, Dan sold it to Fundable, which is a platform that entrepreneurs can use to raise money.)

Dan first heard about Customer Jobs from Eoghan McCabe during Clarity's early years. Eoghan is CEO of Intercom, one of the companies Dan invests in. Dan, intrigued by Eoghan's recommendation, believed Customer Jobs could help him grow Clarity faster:

Once I decided I wanted to learn more about Customer Jobs, the first thing I did was to search Clarity's marketplace. I found some [Customer Jobs] experts and did a few calls. It was really helpful to get real-world experience and advice on how to approach it.

How can Customer Jobs help you do better research? Dan had already been a strong proponent of customer interviews, even before getting into

Customer Jobs. Every week, he would call six customers or so and ask questions such as, "How would you feel if you could no longer use this?" or, "How can we improve Clarity?" But Dan knows that such interviews have limitations. In particular, he understands the difficulties inherent in talking with customers about their habits and that people often want to feel as if they are giving the "correct" answers. "I feel like customers have this really bad habit of lying sometimes," he said. "They'll say, 'Yeah. I love your product. I use it all the time.' Then, you look at the logs, and you realize they haven't logged in once since signing up—so you know it's not true."

Calls with JTBD practitioners helped Dan realize the benefits of framing an interview around what Jobs customers are trying to get done. He did this by changing his questions. Instead of "How would you feel if you could no longer use this?" he asked customers, "Can you tell me about the other solutions you've tried? What did, or didn't you like about each one?" In other words, he shifted from asking broad, individual questions to asking questions aimed at understanding customers' journeys as they searched to find solutions that fit their JTBD. He would then investigate if other customers had similar journeys. Dan said,

> What I love about JTBD is that it really helped me to build a framework for those interviews. Before I became familiar with JTBD, I studied interview questions, extracted pain points, customer language, and all these other things. But when you frame it around the question, 'What is the Job your customer is hiring you to do?' then it really puts a lot of things into perspective and helps you uncover key insights.

What do consumers consider as competition? How do you understand what customers do and don't value in a solution? Dan's new approach to interviewing customers encouraged him to learn about other ways they had tried to get advice. He also wanted to learn if getting expert advice was really what customers were looking for. "Getting expert advice" is just an activity—a solution for a Job. What was the Job itself? What was the emotional motivation to make the customers' lives better? Answering these questions would help him continue to improve and promote Clarity.

To help guide him through these interviews, Dan kept asking himself a few simple but powerful questions:

> What do customers see as competition to Clarity?

What would they spend their money on if they didn't spend it on Clarity?

Have customers set aside a budget for using Clarity or some other solution?

He then asked customers questions such as the following:

What other solutions did you try before deciding on Clarity?

What did, and didn't you like about other solutions you had tried?

If you could no longer use Clarity, what would you use instead?

These questions helped Dan learn what his customers considered as competition to Clarity. He learned that before ending up with Clarity, customers had tried solutions such as joining entrepreneur groups, hiring individual advisers (who take equity), using LinkedIn, and attending conferences. "Understanding how people thought about our product and its competition helped us position it to be different," Dan said. "A lot of people had tried LinkedIn before coming to Clarity. Whereas LinkedIn connects people, it doesn't let them call in real time. It was also interesting to hear that customers considered Clarity as an alternative to attending a conference."

How do you learn what pushes customers to make a change? Dan began to learn two important observations as he talked with customers about the solutions they had used: what his customers did and didn't value in a solution, and what was pushing them to make a change. He found these data by comparing and contrasting all the solutions they had used and asking himself, "What do these solutions have (or what do they not have) in common?" Dan realized that the solutions "use LinkedIn," "hire an adviser," and "attend a conference" had an important aspect in common: entrepreneurs were trying to make a connection with a specific person.

Dan and his team saw that entrepreneurs seeking advice valued the messenger, often more than the message. When it comes to getting advice, it's not just about the content. It has a lot to do with who's delivering it. Dan said,

There's real value in going after that person who is going to motivate you to make a change. It's not just having someone tell you, 'Go get ten sales tomorrow.' It is having billionaire entrepreneur Mark Cuban tell you, 'Go get ten sales tomorrow.'

Dan now knew what was pushing customers to seek a solution: entrepreneurs who were in a slump wanted inspiration from a particular person. Getting advice is just an activity. If the seekers merely wanted advice, they could have read a book or watched a video. They wanted more. They were hoping that someone else's success would rub off on them. This is why they wanted someone they respected to inspire and motivate them to get out of an entrepreneurial slump. That was their emotional motivation to make a change. Making progress with this Job is more valuable to these customers than getting advice. Dan said,

> I've got a list of competitors that tried to build competing solutions. Their marketing and positioning was all about, 'Oh, if you want to talk to this type of person, we have them.' But it was never about a person having the knowledge. It was what [you knew] the person you talked with had accomplished.

How can understanding the customer's moment of struggle help you market a solution? These insights helped Dan and his team make two changes to how they advertised Clarity. Each change would differentiate their solution from what customers considered its competition and help customers realize that Clarity was better. The first change was to emphasize that Clarity would serve its customers on demand. As Dan put it:

> We started saying Clarity gave "on-demand business advice." It was adding the words on demand that differentiated us from LinkedIn—which is an e-mail exchange from which you may or may not get a response. It also differentiated us from attending a conference—you didn't have to wait until the next one came up. We mentioned all that in the copywriting.

The second change was to highlight the fact that using Clarity was cheaper than attending a conference. Dan said, "Understanding what customers considered as competition also helped us position Clarity against the cost of going to a conference. Why invest thousands of dollars in expenses and the cost of a ticket if you can just talk to the speaker today?"

How did the product attract more users and customers? Clarity is a marketplace for connecting buyers (entrepreneurs looking for advice) with sellers (those offering advice). This means that Clarity needed to attract two different groups of people—each with its own motivation for using Clarity.

The motivation for advisers is simple: they want to make money by helping people. The entrepreneurs who use Clarity, however, are different. They want to be motivated and inspired, usually by a particular person. This meant that for its marketplace function to work, Clarity had to find experts whom customers recognized and respected. Dan said,

> Understanding what customers were trying to achieve with LinkedIn and conferences helped us with the supply side of the marketplace. We said to ourselves, "OK, if we recruit experts, we need to recruit a certain type of expert." One of the creative solutions that we came up with was to source experts from SlideShare (a website where conference speakers share their presentations with the public). If you think about it, people who are regarded as inspiring and motivational are those who give creative presentations at conferences. When we wanted to add topics or categories for Clarity, we would source experts who had presentations on SlideShare.

How did Clarity realize its revenue potential? It was Dan's understanding of what customers considered as Clarity's competition that also helped him realize Clarity's revenue potential:

> We learned from customers that their budget for Clarity wasn't coming from the IPO, or from a monthly membership, or from a training budget. It was coming from spending money to go to an event to meet people and to learn.

Dan realized that Clarity wasn't taking money away only from lower-cost alternatives, such as LinkedIn, or from the price of a conference ticket. He learned that Clarity was tapping into the budgets for big-ticket items, such as hiring advisers and consultants, as well as entire budgets for attending conferences, which include airfare, hotels, and meals. This explained why his customers were willing to spend thousands of dollars on calls. This insight helped him understand how valuable his product was to customers. It also helped him understand Clarity's true value in case it was acquired, which it eventually was.

Clarity discovered a silent competitor: anxiety. Nobody comes to Clarity when he or she is having a great day. Dan and his team learned that entrepreneurs were hoping they could get inspired by someone they respected. Without this inspiration, these entrepreneurs would struggle to put into action any advice they were given. This generated demand for the product. But were there any forces that blocked this demand? Dan said, "The biggest competition for us is when a customer chooses to do nothing. I think that's true for a lot of innovations. In Clarity's case, entrepreneurs and innovators continue struggling in the dark. They wouldn't choose to become a self-educator and solve their problem."

Dan began to learn about the anxiety that blocks people from using the product or keeps them from using it more, even when they do decide to reach out to an expert on Clarity:

> One of the questions that I would ask, which was about Clarity as a solution and not their JTBD, was, "What can we change to better meet your needs?" We found a bunch of anxieties around using Clarity. A majority of them were, "What if the expert doesn't answer my question? What's your guarantee? Is the call going to be recorded? What should I do to prep?" That last was one that really threw me off. Both the seekers and experts themselves felt we should teach them how to prepare for a good call.

Dan and his team had taken it for granted that people would be prepared for a call. He assumed that both parties would set up the topic and then have a conversation. This was partly true. Customers had specific questions, but they didn't know how to organize them or what made a question good or bad. Both sides wanted to prep, but they didn't know how.

Another anxiety that both parties shared was the fear of sounding stupid or not putting their best foot forward. What if an expert doesn't have a good answer for a question? What if he or she temporarily forgets the best answer? What if I get nervous and forget my follow-up questions? These anxieties prevented both groups—entrepreneurs and experts—from using Clarity more.

How can you reduce the anxiety customers face when using or buying your product? To fix the problem, Dan and his team added some prep questions and guidelines to the e-mail templates they sent out to notify both parties of a call.

They also provided notes that outlined what a great call looks like and what expectations the parties should have going into the call. Dan said,

> Discovering anxieties like those—that is the interesting part. What I love is thinking, 'Here is the problem, and here is the anxiety point. How do we solve it in a way that's elegant, simple, and doesn't confuse the interface?' That was always the fun part for me.

How can JTBD be used to research new features? As Dan became more familiar with JTBD, he began to develop his own tools and processes that would help him apply JTBD principles to improve Clarity. One such process was aimed at helping his team quickly validate ideas for new features.

Before committing to developing a feature, the Clarity team wanted to make sure the problem they intended to solve was actually one that customers had. The best way to learn this was to find out if customers had tried to solve the problem before. Dan said, "An interview about how customers had tried to solve a problem in the past was more like a feature-usage time line than a purchase decision."

An example of a feature the Clarity team chose not to build was one that saved search results when users looked for experts on Clarity's marketplace.

> We asked customers questions like, "Have you ever tried to save results when you searched for an expert?" If they said no, then we'd move on. We then asked, "Do you have a browser bookmarklet? Which ones?" Then, they would say, "Evernote, Buffer…" It would provide so much context outside of the feature. It was more about how the customer had tried to solve their problems in the past.

So, Dan's team decided not to build the browser bookmarklet. They didn't think it delivered enough value because the problem it solved wasn't one their customers had struggled with. Dan said,

> A lot of people—especially if they're committed or already invested in a solution—are looking for that confirmation bias that it's something they should do. It's a different question to ask customers how they solved the problem in the past. I could ask them, "Hey, what do you think of this?" They might say, "Oh,

it's prettier. It works great." But that's not really answering the question we're asking. We want to know, "Are you going to use it? Are you struggling to make progress? Have you tried to solve this in the past? Do you want to hire someone or something to solve this Job to be Done?" If the answer is no, then cool. We write that down and move on.

How does JTBD help innovators? Dan appreciates the focus JTBD puts on exploring customer motivation. He also wishes more companies would do that rather than "spy" on customers.

> I think the biggest thing that Jobs [JTBD] encourages people to do, which I'm a big fan of, is to stop spying on customers and start talking with customers. I feel that way especially with software because we have the analytics and the geeks who are building the software; they're all about tracking and logging and all these data…I always give the analogy of being a retail shop owner and hiding in the back room and trying to learn from your customers by watching the closed-circuit television.

> You could watch [customers] come in, walk around your store, pick up things, put them down, try things on…or you could just walk out and ask them, "Hey, what brought you in here today? What are you looking for? What other places did you try in the past?" Talking to customers about their motivations is where you're going to learn the most.

WHAT'S THE JTBD?

From the data Dan has given us, I'd say that the desire for progress is as follows:

> More about: getting out of a rut, making a connection with someone whose accomplishments I respect, being inspired, being motivated to act, feeling like I'm on the right path, having confidence in what I'm doing, having success rub off on me, on demand.

> Less about: getting expert advice, talking with an expert, giving away equity, having a video chat with a mentor, e-mailing a

mentor, mentoring, meeting other entrepreneurs, seeing a mentor live.

Here are some possible descriptions of the one or more Jobs to be Done Clarity is hired for:

Help me get out of an innovation slump with inspirational advice from someone whom I respect.

Give me the motivation to act with a kick in the butt from someone I respect.

Take away the anxiety of making a big decision with assurance from someone else whose has been in a similar position.

These work for me because they don't describe an activity or task. They describe the motivation that comes before engaging in an activity (i.e., using a solution). Also, notice how these descriptions can be used to describe the other solutions customers had tried in the past (e.g., attending a conference, giving away advisory shares, and using LinkedIn). This is important because a JTBD either doesn't change or does so slowly. If a description of a JTBD works for solutions from one hundred years ago, it'll probably work for solutions one hundred years into the future.

PUT IT TO WORK

Dan's case study is a great introduction to Customer Jobs. Here are some suggestions to help you get started today with applying Customer Jobs thinking.

Ask customers about what they've done, not just what they want. Confirm it if you can. Customers will often tell us what we want to hear, even if it's partially (or completely) untrue. Customers may tell you that they use your product "all the time," but they really use it only intermittently. Also, people build easy-to-remember narratives between themselves and the products they use. Phenomena like this are why it's tricky to ask customers, "What do you want?" and "How can we make things better?"[21]

The answer for these problems is to talk with customers about what they actually did, not just about what they say they want. What were their revealed preferences, not just their stated preferences? Even the answers about actual action taken won't be 100 percent accurate, but they will be a great deal more reliable than their answers to what–if questions.[22]

Understanding how customers have solved problems is a crucial part of understanding their JTBD. Not only does it help you understand what customers expect from a product, but it also helps you design features for new products.

Ask the right questions to learn how your customers view competition. Accurate models of competition can come from only customers. Any model of competition that doesn't come from them is invalid. One way of getting the information you need to build a correct model of competition is through customer interviews and surveys. Ask them questions such as the following:

> What other solutions did you consider before trying the product?

> What other solutions have you actually used?

> If the product wasn't available to you, what would you have done instead?

> What solutions have the people you know tried or used?

Learn what kind of progress customers are seeking. What's their emotional motivation (JTBD)? Use that to segment competition. Dan learned that Clarity's customers saw its competition as attending conferences, using LinkedIn, and hiring advisers. These solutions have vastly different functionality and qualities. However, from the customers' point of view, they appeal to the same aspiration: "Get me out of an entrepreneurial slump with motivational advice from someone whom I respect." Discover your customers' motivation through comparing and contrasting the solutions that they consider as competition:

> What do the various solutions have in common? What is different about them?

> What did, or didn't the customers like about each solution?

> What would customers do if they couldn't use their existing solution for their JTBD?

What would the consequences be?

How are they expecting life to be better once they have the right solution for a JTBD?

These types of questions help you understand two things: what customers are struggling with now, and how they hope life will be better when they have the right solution. Put these two together, and you'll have their JTBD.

Ask yourself, "From which budget will my product take away money?" Also ask, "When customers start using my product, what will they stop using?" Dan learned that his customers were willing to spend thousands of dollars on Clarity calls. This number didn't come from looking at how much other "talk to an expert" products cost. He learned this by understanding that his product—from the customers' point of view—was replacing the entire budget of going to a conference.

I've noted that when it comes to solutions for a JTBD, customers can use only one at a time. When they start using one solution, they have to stop using something else. This helps you understand what the competition is. It also helps you gauge how to price your product properly and figure your revenue potential. Should you charge less or more? You have two big factors to consider: the amount customers are already accustomed to spending on a solution for a JTBD, and the intensity of their desire to change. The more they hope to change, the more they are willing to pay.

Create better marketing material by speaking to your customers' JTBD. Dan Martell described Clarity as "on-demand business advice." He also featured access to experts whom customers would recognize. He also positioned Clarity as an alternative to going to a conference: Why spend the time and money going to a conference? Talk with the speaker today! Both of these messages spoke to customers' motivations and distinguished Clarity as unique.

Talk with customers to learn what messages connect with them. It can be as simple as asking them to describe why they like your product. Sometimes, you have to probe deeper and ask them questions such as, "Before you bought our product, how did you know it was right for you?" The best promotional material, however, comes from speaking directly to their desire for progress.

Focus on delivering emotional progress (getting a Job Done). Don't focus solely on functionality. Dan mentioned a list of people who had tried to create solutions similar to Clarity. They failed, and Clarity won because Dan designed and marketed it in a way that spoke to customers' emotional motivation. The Clarity clones thought of themselves as "talk to an expert" products; they were focusing on functionality, activities, and tasks. But Dan focused on the emotional quality—that is, customers' JTBD. He knew that customers wanted to be motivated and inspired by someone whom they respect. This made Clarity stand out, and it's why Fundable acquired it. Clarity's former competitors, however, have already been forgotten.

Your guiding star in understanding your customers' JTBD is their motivation to better their lives. Focus on that. Focusing on functionality will distract you.

5 CASE STUDY: ANTHONY AND FORM THEATRICALS

What's the JTBD?
Put it to work

What progress might someone use theater for? I had never asked this question before, but Anthony Francavilla had. For the past few years, Anthony has been applying Customer Jobs principles to figure out the answers to that question. Theater has been around for thousands of years. Shouldn't we know the reasons why people attend the theater? Maybe. But maybe not.

Anthony has managed and produced theater for ten years. In 2012, he cofounded Form Theatricals, whose mission is to help productions grow and be successful. This is particularly challenging in the theater world. Many productions are run by actors or writers who often don't have much business experience. They also have little to no experience innovating around customer motivation. This is where Anthony and Form Theatricals come in.

Customer Jobs has helped Anthony figure out how to learn what really matters to theatergoers; what customers do and don't consider as competition to theater; and how a theater production could improve its shows for patrons, increase profits from ticket sales, develop new types of theater products, and reduce the cost of operating a show.

Why look into Customer Jobs? Anthony knew that interviewing theater patrons was the key to improving a show. But what's the best way to interview people about a show they've just seen? To find out, he sought advice from someone who specializes in interviewing customers. Anthony said,

> I got together with this guy, Boris, who specializes in ethnographic interviewing. I said to him, "I have this problem with a client. People don't like the show, but it's selling well. I want to interview customers, but I don't know what I should be asking them about." He said I could talk to them and try to find out what Job these patrons are trying to get Done. He asked me if I had heard about Customer Jobs. I told him I hadn't. He explained it to me. Then, he told me about some sources online where I could learn more. I also signed up for the Customer Jobs Meetup that's run here in New York.

After looking into Customer Jobs, a bit more and learning about some of the tools associated with the principles, it didn't take long for Anthony to start gathering powerful insights.

Studying what customers consider as competition helps you reveal what pushes them to change. It also helps reveal their JTBD. Anthony applied some Customer Jobs thinking to his next client: a children's theater company. To begin, he interviewed parents who had taken their children to the company's show. He wanted to know why they chose this particular show. Did they consider any other activities for their children besides attending the theater? He told me, "We interviewed a bunch of parents. We learned that the options they had considered [as alternatives to attending the theater] ranged from going to The LEGO Movie and buying the LEGO video game to signing their children up to clubs—like the Girl Scouts."

This was a story Anthony kept hearing. Parents were considering a wide array of options as alternatives to taking their children to this particular theater show. Or, in Customer Jobs terms, he learned exactly what parents considered as competition for their JTBD. These customers surely used the theater for other Jobs in other circumstances. But in this case, what Job were they hoping to get Done by bringing their children to this show?

To help him answer this question, Anthony applied Customer Jobs' idea of "contrast reveals value." He talked with these parents about what they did or didn't like about the other options they had considered. What can the theater do for them that an alternative solution—such as the Girl Scouts—can't? He also asked these parents about what they did immediately after the shows. Did they have family discussions about them? What were those discussions like? After talking with numerous parents, he began to see a distinct pattern. "We found out that part of the Job these parents are trying to get done—when it comes to entertainment and activities for their kids—was that they wanted help teaching their kids how to be independent…while also reinforcing that they are a member of a team."

How do you go about making product changes when you understand the customers' desire for progress? Anthony brought these insights to his client. Together, they decided to rewrite parts of the play. They kept most of the content the same, but they added a story arc wherein the hero works with the characters around him to solve a problem. This would give parents a talking point with their children about the importance of working with others. Anthony said,

It's interesting to me because helping writers understand what Job parents are using their play for is more powerful than saying to them, "Write a movie, or write a play that a nine-year-old will like." When we know that parents have a Job that involves their desire to teach their children life lessons in an entertaining way, we can work with our clients to help them craft their content better. When we present it as a Job to be Done, the artist has a lot of leeway around what the story should do.

For Anthony's client to sell more tickets to these parents, the performances had to help parents make progress against their JTBD, which included their aspiration to be responsible parents, as well as becoming better at teaching life lessons to their children. This needed to be done in a way that their kids would enjoy. The performance also had to do this better than what parents considered as competition—namely, other plays, movies, video games, and clubs.

Anthony wouldn't have got the same depth of insight had he interviewed parents only about what they did and didn't like about the play. Had he done that, he would have ended up getting a lot of feedback about how to make the play better—but only in comparison with other plays. With a Customer Jobs approach to understanding competition, he was now learning how theater compared with other solutions customers had tried.

What do we gain from digging deeper into the JTBD? Anthony wasn't satisfied with just the one insight that these parents wanted help teaching their children life lessons. He wanted to dig deeper into their motivation. Were there other ways they were hoping that theater would make their lives better? He said,

> One of the things we figured out was that parents want to have shared experiences with their kids. That's not necessarily understood by the producers of theater and movies. On the surface, it doesn't seem like a shared experience. Theater productions often see the dynamic of a play as "Let's just go sit in a dark room and watch this together." What we learned—and what a lot people don't realize—is that the shared experience actually happens after the show. It's when everyone goes out for dinner and they talk about the movie or the play they just saw.

This insight about shared experiences prompted Anthony to ask parents other questions. What were other shared experiences they engaged in with their children? How did theater fit into those?

> I interviewed this father about how he, his wife, and his child would pick what they were going to watch on TV. They were basically engaged in rhetoric; they would each debate what they wanted to watch. They'd go back and forth, to the point that sometimes the debate would end with them all deciding to just go their separate ways and reading their own books. They wanted to have a shared experience—to the point that the debate itself became the shared experience—and they didn't end up watching anything on TV.

By comparing and contrasting how families had and felt about shared experiences, Anthony could begin to understand what customers did and didn't like about each solution. What made discussion about what to watch on TV so successful? What things didn't families like about it? What were family discussions like after the family saw a play together? Were these discussions about life lessons or about other things, such as the performances of the actors? How could a theater show promote better conversations at home?

Answers to these questions helped Anthony understand that these parents wanted to make family life better through engaging and educational discussions with their children. These conversations were a bonding experience. This was exactly the kind of direction his client needed. It helped the children's theater company make script adjustments, so its plays could act as vehicles for family conversations.

How many Jobs might an innovation be used for? Anthony's interviews with families had been successful. Understanding what Jobs they were using theater for helped him provide guidance for his client. He decided to continue Customer Jobs research with his other clients.

The next few shows he worked on were drama pieces with more serious subject matter—definitely not for kids. Patrons were usually individuals or small groups of friends. What Job might these people be using theater for? Anthony said,

> We interviewed a banker who went to a show by himself. He said, "I love these weird off-off-Broadway plays." As we dived deeper into what that meant, we began to realize that an important

part of the theater experience was who else is in the audience. That's what one group of customers was looking for. They would say, "I want to hang out with artists more." Others would say, "It's just amazing. I don't normally sit in a room and have an experience with a group of diverse people like that."

This is how Anthony began to discover another Job that people use theater for: it was about being a part of, or dipping their toes into, a different community. Very often, these customers had careers that weren't arts related, such as banking or law. He would hear comments such as "I like these productions that are a bit out there," "I like going because there are artists in the audience. They're talking about art," or "I don't have a job in the arts, but I love the arts. I want to be involved in that kind of scene." For many of these patrons, going to these shows was their only opportunity to engage with a diverse group of people. They liked the arts. They wanted to be involved in that community. Anthony said,

> That was a very impactful insight. A lot of times, the theater will try to sell you the idea that it's like a movie—but on stage. You can't compete with that. Theater is more expensive. It's sometimes super-inconvenient to attend a show. I have Netflix. If I want to watch a movie, I can hit a button, and there is a movie.

> Figuring out what Job live entertainment solves for people in the twenty-first century is exciting. We've learned that, yes, it is entertainment, but it's also about this idea of community. It's something that you're going to enjoy with other people. Maybe there will also be drinks, food, a lively atmosphere—all that kind of stuff. That's something that a theater can take and use to build up a new business model for the twenty-first century—as opposed to this idea that there's going to be a celebrity in the show. Tickets for those shows are two hundred and fifty dollars. There's a very limited audience for that.

How can Customer Jobs help you reimagine existing products? With these new insights, Anthony and his clients were able to create a new type of theater experience: a theater subscription product. When people buy these subscriptions, each person is put into a specific cohort of customers. Shows are picked out for these customers. Over several months, this same group of people sees the same shows and engages in social events around the show. Anthony said,

These patrons valued this idea of inclusiveness. It is important for us to help theater productions understand that patrons are looking for an inclusive experience. This meant making the subscription affordable. It's easier for a banker to pay five hundred dollars for a few shows than it is for many artists. We solved this problem by offering multiple payment options. You could spread the price over months or pay for the whole subscription up front.

How can Customer Jobs help you avoid wasting resources by building features that customers don't care about? Anthony didn't help his clients by only suggesting to them what they should add to a show. He also made suggestions on what to take out of it.

One of Anthony's clients had a production that featured an after-the-show tour of the stage for anyone who attended. It was something the producers of the show were proud of. But did patrons enjoy it? As he interviewed patrons after the show, he learned that most of them hadn't known about the tour when they bought their tickets. They had simply chosen the show because tickets were being sold at a discount. He said,

> The majority of these patrons learned about the show and the discount on the day of the show. For some of them, it had been a last-minute decision. They'd be discussing with friends what to do for the evening. Should they just go to a bar? A comedy club? But when they noticed the discounted theater tickets, they then chose to buy tickets. It could be an hour or two before the show started.

Of all the people he interviewed, only one or two knew that the set tour was going to happen. Anthony's client had assumed that theater patrons were interested in access to the actors and seeing how the show worked. As it happened, almost no one who bought a ticket knew about the tour. The tour hadn't been part of these patrons' purchase criteria, so it didn't help explain why they were hiring the show. Anthony said,

> We learned that people were not hiring the show to get access to the actors and set after the show. Finding that piece of information was very valuable. The after-show tour was expensive to maintain, and it wasn't something patrons were particularly interested in. The Job for those patrons was about entertainment and having a shared experience with their friends and significant others.

In this case, the producers had overengineered the show. They had designed the show based on what they valued—a tour of the set—instead of what their customers valued—having a shared, fun experience with their friends. After gaining these insights, Anthony worked with the producers to discontinue the set tours. While experimentation is good, it has to be within the constraints of the Job that customers are hiring the show for. The new thinking freed up the show's designers to focus on what they were doing right and make that better.

How does anxiety stop customers from buying your product? Is there really such a thing as an "impulse purchase"? Similar to tickets for airplanes, sporting events, and movies, theater tickets are worthless after the event starts. Seats are perishable inventory. This posed an interesting challenge for Anthony and his clients. To help him figure out how his clients could sell more tickets, he began interviewing customers to learn more about the key events that sped up or slowed down a decision to buy a ticket. Were there any anxieties about attending a particular show? If so, how could a theater production solve this problem? Anthony said,

> For each customer, we mapped out a time line of the events that led up to their ticket purchase. We began to hear the same things over and over again. Things like, a husband reads a magazine with his friends at work—that's where he'll first find out about a play. He'll e-mail his wife about it. She'll respond with a comment like, "Seems interesting. I like that it's a horror-themed play set in Spanish. I like horror." But when bad reviews for it come out, they start to doubt if they'll like it. But they still keep an eye on the show. Then, maybe a week later, they'll learn about the discount. At that minute, they're pushed over the edge and buy the tickets.

Anthony discovered two insights here: some anxieties prevent customers from buying tickets to a show, and tickets that seem to be impulse purchases sometimes aren't.

The majority of customers who bought a ticket through a discount did so on the day of the show, but that doesn't mean these were impulse purchases. In the backs of their minds, these customers already had specific shows they wanted to see. But what was holding them back from buying the tickets? Anxiety. They'd first be excited about a show's concept, but if reviews weren't positive, they'd hold off. The discount, however, could compress the purchase time line. It eased anxiety and caused potential patrons to buy.

Can Customer Jobs theory gather new insights about a medium that is thousands of years old? As the competition for theater changes with the advance of technology, it's important to focus on the Jobs that customers hire theater for. Many parents use it as a way to help them have the types of conversations they want with their children and to help them teach life lessons. For those who want to expand and bring diversity to their social circles, community and diversity are critical.

Anthony's application of JTBD principles and focusing on customer motivation have enabled him to innovate within a medium that is thousands of years old.

WHAT'S THE JTBD?

This case study reveals different directions of progress that people hope to make using theater. This would explain why there are so many different types of theater shows. Some big themes associated with Jobs to Be Done I heard include using shared experiences to create or strengthen bonds with family and friends, parents teaching their children life lessons, and adding excitement to your social life by getting involved with people whom you normally wouldn't interact with.

The clearest JTBD I heard was related to parents' desires. They wanted to teach their children how to be independent, while also understanding how to work with others. This works for solutions such as video games, movies, clubs like the Girl Scouts, and attending the theater. This case study had some great data about customer motivation; however, I still have questions about these parents' motivations:

> What are some of the consequences of not teaching their children life lessons?

> Is there something in these parents' lives that is pushing them to make a change now, or are they deciding to be proactive and avoid feeling guilty in the future?

> Does having conversations about life lessons relate to anything else going on in the lives of these parents or children? What about school or interactions with their friends?

What other solutions do parents couple with theater to make progress?

How will parents know their Job is Done? That is, when do they know they are making progress and things are getting better?

I would have a better idea of what progress parents are trying to make once I had answers to questions such as these.

PUT IT TO WORK

How do you persuade teammates or management to change a product? Frame design challenges as a JTBD. Innovators like to solve problems; we don't like being told what to do. I find it's best to motivate a team by presenting them with problems to solve in the form of a customer's JTBD.

Dig deeper when you tap into a struggle or aspiration. How have customers tried to solve it before? Anthony discovered that parents had a desire for shared experiences with their kids. But what does shared experiences mean? It turns out that a shared experience is most important after the show. This insight gave Anthony the idea to talk with other patrons about their shared experiences. What made a shared experience successful? How had the patrons tried to have shared experiences?

When customers describe a struggle or aspiration, don't make assumptions about what they mean; rather, unpack what they're saying. Ask for specific examples. If they describe a struggle, how do they imagine life being better once they solve it? If they describe an aspiration, what are the consequences if they can't achieve it? The answers will help you make design, marketing, and business decisions.

Discover what customers value. Learn their expectations at the moment of purchase and/or first use and avoid overengineering solutions. Anthony had a client who offered a costly after-the-show tour of the set. However, he learned that almost no patrons were aware that the tour was being offered, so it didn't affect their purchase decisions. This made it safe to remove tours from the show. This reduced costs of production, and it increased profits.

A great deal of waste happens when solutions are developed with features that customers don't value. Customers value the progress a feature may deliver, not the feature itself.

If you have an existing product, engage in an audit to determine which features don't help customers make progress toward their JTBD. If you're about to create a new feature, make sure it delivers progress and, more importantly, helps you increase profits. You might learn just as one of Anthony's clients did—namely, that you're spending money to support features that customers don't find valuable.

Determine if anxiety is a competitor. If it is, find ways of reducing it. You should attack the anxieties in choosing and using a product with the same fervor as attacking a competing product. If customers have anxiety over the cost-value relationship of your product, offer a discount. If customers experience anxiety in using your product, find a way to make your product less intimidating. Anthony attacked the former by offering discounts on the day of the show. He attacked the latter by offering drinks as "liquid courage" for theater patrons to feel more comfortable mingling with one another.

Be suspicious of the "impulse purchase" concept. No purchase is random. Anthony discovered that many customers purchased tickets on the day of—or even an hour or two before—the shows. But that doesn't mean that these were impulse purchases. Many patrons had already decided they wanted to see a show; they had reservations about paying full price for a show that had received mixed reviews. A lowered price helped ease their anxiety about paying for a show that might not be very good.

Talk with customers about how they came to choose your product for their JTBD. They might claim that their purchase of a USB charging cable was "just an impulse purchase while I was waiting in line." However, when you dig deeper, you might learn that they were about to go on a trip and wanted to take an inexpensive charging cable with them in case it got lost during their travels.

6 CASE STUDY: MORGAN AND YOURGROCER

What's the JTBD?
Put it to work

Morgan Ranieri was fed up. Getting home from work at seven o'clock at night meant he couldn't get the groceries he wanted, for the stores he wanted to shop at were closed by then. Instead, he had to settle for the supermarket chains around Melbourne, Australia, where Morgan lives. I say "settle" because the food quality at these supermarkets isn't very good. Shopping there also meant he wasn't supporting family businesses, which was something he liked to do.

Sensing that he shared this struggle with other people, he teamed up with his colleague Bandith and created YourGrocer. The concept for YourGrocer was simple: have your groceries delivered to you from local, high-quality food shops.

Over the next few months, Morgan and Bandith did some tests to see if the YourGrocer concept could work. They investigated what the competition might be, what logistics would need to be in place, and how many local shops were interested in partnering with them, and they even did some preliminary testing with a few customers to get feedback.

Their tests told them that an opportunity did exist. However, to grow their business, Morgan and Bandith needed someone with more technical expertise to join the team. Morgan met Francisco (Frankie) Trindade at a local Meetup. Morgan said, "Over the next month or so, we began speed dating, in a sense—getting to know one another before deciding to work together."

In this case study, we learn how Customer Jobs helped Morgan build a consensus among team members, what customers did and didn't value in a solution, find the right marketing messages, how it helped first-time customers switch to Morgan's product, and how he could reduce churn.

Customer Jobs helps you persuade others that an opportunity exists.
Frankie wanted to make sure an opportunity existed before he joined YourGrocer as its third cofounder. This is when Frankie introduced Morgan to Customer Jobs. Frankie told Morgan that he wanted to spend more time learning what Job(s) customers would use YourGrocer for. He especially

wanted to do this before writing any of the software that would power the business. Morgan said,

> It was Frankie who introduced me and Bandith to Jobs (Customer Jobs). Actually, the first thing Frankie did when he joined YourGrocer was to make sure we all understood the principles of Customer Jobs. We spent a week learning about it and figuring out how we would interview customers. All of us learning about Customer Jobs, and then interviewing twenty customers together, was a great way to induct him as YourGrocer's third cofounder.

How does your team benefit from doing Customer Jobs research together? The newly formed YourGrocer team gained an unexpected benefit of doing Customer Jobs research together. As Morgan said,

> This shared learning experience really helped bring us together. We developed a shared understanding of what the business needed to be—which was missing in the beginning. At the start, we all had very different ideas about what customers were struggling with and how we should solve it. I was the typical visionary cofounder who has the next five years planned out in my head—which is very dangerous. But Frankie didn't make many assumptions. He wanted to take it one step at a time. His middle name should be "Pragmatic": Frankie Pragmatic.
>
> Interviewing about twenty customers got me, as a business cofounder, and Frankie, as a new technical cofounder, on to the same page.

Are data about "types" of people information or misinformation? The first aha moment for the YourGrocer team was when they realized that their customers didn't match the assumed demographic. Morgan said,

> We had an assumption about what our customer demographic was—or the idea of who our target customer was. The reality turned out to be quite different. We thought we were creating a business for young professionals who wanted to buy groceries online. It turns out, almost every single one of our customers was a young family—typically a young mom with a couple of kids at home.

At first, the YourGrocer team created the business out of their own need—that is, a way for busy young professionals to buy groceries online. But because most of the company's customers were young families, the team needed to adjust. "It just turned out that the type of customers we were targeting at first [young professionals] didn't really work too well for our product, but this other group of customers [parents] was ripe for it."

How do struggling moments arise? What is it like to be pushed to change? Morgan and his team had now picked up on a group of struggling customers. The next step was to learn how and why these people were struggling. What was the struggling moment? This meant that Morgan first needed to talk with these customers about the different ways they had purchased groceries before. Morgan began to uncover the triggering events that would push these customers from one solution to another.

> The push that eventually led our customers to YourGrocer often began a couple of years in the past. They'd start off shopping at the shops they liked. Then they'd have their first child. Getting around to these shops with one kid was difficult, but they could deal with it. But once they had their second child, that would really change things. Having a second kid made it almost impossible to get to the local shops they wanted. That's when they switched from their local shops to buying at the two big suppliers here.

As a customer's family grew, more of his or her time was dedicated to caregiving. It also made traveling to multiple food shops difficult. This would lead these families to consider other ways of getting their groceries, such as at supermarkets.

Discovering these triggering events helped Morgan understand how demand was being generated and how it pushed these parents to seek a solution. This helped him get an idea of how these parents were trying to make their lives better—that is, what Job they were trying to get Done.

What is it like to learn what customers do and don't like about solutions they've tried? Next, Morgan had to learn how these parents had already tried to solve their problem—namely, how to get groceries when they had children to take care of. Comparing and contrasting these solutions would help him understand what these customers did and didn't value in a solution.

In particular, these parents complained about cost, poor-quality food, and not being able to choose foods they wanted.

> The big supermarkets do fresh produce badly. The other local delivery suppliers that do fresh produce well are expensive. Some of them even have these subscription models where you get a preselected assortment of groceries. Customers can't pick and choose what they want, when they want it. Our customers didn't like that. They were getting a bunch of stuff they didn't want, not using it, having it all go bad, and getting frustrated by that. Often, all these issues with other services had been going on for some time. They were just putting up with it. Then, we came along. It was just what they had been waiting for.

What are examples of things customers value? Before starting YourGrocer, Morgan and his team already had a pretty good idea of what the business would be: home delivery from the quality shops his customers loved. Now they were filling in any blanks and confirming their assumptions of the value that YourGrocer should deliver. Here's what they were learning:

> Convenience had become these customers' top priority. They used to value food quality the most, but traveling with their kids to multiple stores proved too difficult for them. This pushed them to trade food quality for convenience.[23]

> After convenience, they wanted to be able to choose foods they wanted. This ruled out services that delivered to the home but didn't allow buyers to choose their own food options.

> Quality got pushed to the bottom. Ultimately, these customers ended up choosing food from supermarkets. While supermarkets offered the lowest-quality foods, they ranked the highest on convenience and selection.

How does JTBD help you create a message that connects with customers? The YourGrocer team members were confident that they now understood what the customers valued and that the team could deliver this value. The next step was to figure out a message that would connect with customers. Once again, customer interviews helped Morgan and his team figure this out.

In the beginning, we didn't know which messages would stick with customers. We would say, "It's good to shop locally, because it's good for the environment. It's better food. It's better priced. It's convenient. It's local shops. It's good for your community." We were throwing out half a dozen different messages out there without knowing which ones would persuade customers to try us.

Morgan solved this problem by asking his customers JTBD-style questions, such as "What stood out to you about us?" As he did so, he began to gain rich details about customers' motivations.

One thing we really like about Customer Jobs is that you want to learn from customers what they've done in the past. You're not just asking customers their opinion at the time you're talking with them or through a survey. We would ask them, "What did you tell your friends about YourGrocer?" Or, better yet, "Can you show me the text in your phone that you sent your friend about us?"

Morgan's customers had no problem pulling out their phones and showing him the text messages they had sent to others about YourGrocer, as well as any Facebook posts they had made about shopping with it. In those messages, Morgan saw customers express what they felt was valuable about YourGrocer. He learned that the messages they sent to other people were about getting groceries from a store:

We knew that customers wanted quality foods. But just saying we offered quality wasn't enough. We learned that customers trusted our message of quality only because of the local stores we featured on our site and advertisements. Other messages didn't stick with them—being good for the environment, our competitive pricing, the ease of use when compared to other delivery services. All that kind of stuff wasn't really standing out to our customers. It turned out, they were buying from us because they recognized the stores that we featured on our website.

This is when the YourGrocer team honed their advertising message. It combined convenience, variety, and quality into one statement: "Online grocery shopping and same-day home delivery from the local shops you love."

What anxieties do first-time customers experience? What might prevent customers from using your product? So far, Morgan has learned about how important convenience is to his customers. Just how important this was became even more salient when he talked with customers about the first time they tried to use YourGrocer for delivery. He said,

> We learned about this one anxiety: a lot of people came to the site and had trouble trying to figure out how YourGrocer would fit into their lives. We kept hearing comments such as, "I just don't know when my groceries are going to get delivered." This struck us as odd because we give really flexible delivery options.

This anxiety didn't make sense to Morgan and his team. They offered flexible delivery hours, so why were customers commenting about not knowing when their groceries would be delivered? The answer lay in customers' shopping habits and expectations. Morgan said, "It turns out that customers had this obstacle in their buying path. They decided what groceries to buy only after they'd figure out when they'd get the delivery. We had it reversed: you would pick your groceries first and then decide when to have them delivered."

> First-time customers coming to the site already had an idea of how YourGrocer was going to work. They had a habit or expectation of coming to a site, finding out how soon they could get a delivery, and then deciding what to buy. When this expectation was violated, they became frustrated and anxious. At this point, they would abandon trying out YourGrocer.[24]

To fix this problem, YourGrocer adjusted the checkout process. It asked customers to pick a delivery window first and then walked them through the grocery-selection process. "That helped," Morgan said. "We saw conversions go up after that."

What habits prevent customers from making progress? Can customers' habits be competition? Anxiety wasn't the only emotional force the YourGrocer team members would face. They also had to navigate customers' existing habits. Morgan said,

> Dealing with customers' existing habits was definitely a challenge with repeat-purchase customers. They had this habit around being able to duck down to the local store when they ran out of a key ingredient while cooking. Then, while they were at the store,

they'd pick up extra groceries. In this case, they wouldn't need to come back to us for another two weeks. Sometimes they'd fall out of the buying cycle, and we'd lose them as customers. Habits like these are our biggest competition.

If Morgan wanted to keep customers coming back, he needed to make sure that customers developed new habits around using YourGrocer. He couldn't focus on only the outcomes customers were looking for. He had to think holistically about the customers' JTBD. Customers didn't just want their groceries delivered; they wanted a solution they could use to make their lives better.

So, how did Morgan and his team solve it? They focused on helping customers become more successful at using their product.

> We get people to set up regular orders with us. We set up e-mail triggers to help remind them that they might need something. The first one goes out three days after getting your first delivery. We send you an e-mail saying, "Hey, do you need a top-up on anything? Here's a free delivery of any size so that you can top up with us." Seven days after your last purchase, we e-mail you again and ask, "Do you know how easy it is to repeat last week's order? You can just click this button and get everything delivered again."

These e-mails are part of YourGrocer's efforts to help customers become better meal planners. This is important to note because customers aren't consciously joining YourGrocer to become better meal planners. It wasn't an outcome that customers were seeking; however, meal planning is what customers have to be able to do if they want to use YourGrocer for their JTBD.

What progress are customers trying to make? Morgan and his team came to understand their customers' JTBD by combining their own intuition with what they learned through customer interviews.

> An important part of our customers' Job to be Done is, "Give me a way to provide quality food for my family without the stress of running around." The phrase "YourGrocer does the running around for me" came up quite a bit during the interviews. Before YourGrocer was available to them, if they wanted to go to these local shops, they had to be willing to deal with running around to

these different stores—and deal with the hassle of having their kids in tow.

Morgan had the first part of the JTBD: his customers were struggling to get quality groceries without all the stress. Next, it was time for him to understand how customers were expecting their lives to be better when they had the right solution. What would it be like when this Job was Done?

> YourGrocer helps families get back their Saturday mornings and weekends. With us, they can now buy good food for their family without having to sacrifice their Saturday mornings or weekends visiting all these different stores. That's the trade-off they were struggling with before. If they wanted quality food for their family, they'd have to give up some family time so they could go shopping. If they didn't want to give up family time, then they'd have to deal with poor-quality food from the supermarkets.

How can you beat the competition? Eliminate the need for the customer to make a trade-off. YourGrocer wins because it does what every great innovation does—that is, it helps customers break a constraint. Using YourGrocer means no longer choosing between quality food for the family and quality time with the family. Morgan said,

> Once the convenience trade-off was equalized—YourGrocer makes local shopping just as convenient as using a supermarket—then other trade-offs, such as quality and supporting the community, became the differentiators. That's what sets us above the supermarkets. That's the real progress that people are able to make with us.

WHAT'S THE JTBD?

From the data Morgan has given us, I'd say that the struggle for progress is as follows:

> More about: My family having quality food, taking away the stress from grocery shopping, more family time, convenience.

> Less about: Grocery shopping online/supermarket /local shop, supporting the local community.

Again, any kind of task or activity associated with grocery shopping is just a solution for a JTBD—it's not part of the JTBD itself. I know people who employ housemaids to keep the household fridge stocked with food and groceries. That entails no shopping at all—you pay someone else to take care of it. For those who can't afford or don't like that solution, grocery-delivery service is a nice alternative.

The progression of solutions in this case study helps us understand what customers do and don't value. In the beginning, parents were fine visiting multiple shops. They were willing to trade convenience for food quality. But when their family grew, saving time and reducing stress became more important to them. This is how we know that their desire to evolve, their JTBD, is heavily related to finding a way to solve that stress and to save time.

This case study also demonstrates how customer needs or wants change over time and don't belong to the customer. We may think we're measuring a need, but we're really just measuring what a customer does or doesn't like about a particular solution. We must keep in mind that a "need" represents an interaction between the customer, their desire for progress, and whatever product they've hired for their JTBD. If one of those parts changes, then customers' needs will change along with it.

Put It to Work

Don't depend on demographics. At first, Morgan thought he was making a product for young, urban professionals. This demographic certainly did represent some of his customers; however, it turned out that his most dedicated customers were families. Not only that, they almost always had two or more young children.

We can learn from this that demographic thinking can be misleading. It was the customers' situation—not personal characteristics—that determined why they bought. Sometimes, you do have to collect and use demographic data. They can help you when you buy ads and develop promotional material. If you need to develop an ad for video or print, you'll have to cast actors and set a scene. That means making concrete decisions on what those people should look like, what they do, and where they are. However, these data shouldn't be used as a basis for product and marketing decisions. They are corollary data, not causal data. Use demographic data only as a guide or hint to help you find JTBD data.

Know the difference between customers who switch because they are unhappy with your solution and those who switch because changing life circumstances prompt a redefinition of progress. In Morgan's case study, the local food shops may or may not have known why their customers stopped shopping with them. Was it because supermarkets offered more selection? Was it about quality? Was it about price? As it happens, none of these applied. These customers switched because they needed more convenience.

Let's slow down and think about this. Notice something important and subtle here. By only observing customers, these businesses would have deduced that some switched to supermarkets. In response, these shops might have been tempted to change their businesses to be more like supermarkets. A butcher shop might think it should offer a wider selection of foods or lower its prices. Yet these things were not why the shops were losing customers. It was about convenience.

Next, imagine that these shops did learn that they were losing customers because of convenience. What should they do about it? This is a turning point where many businesses go terribly wrong. The knee-jerk reaction for many businesses in this position would be to figure out ways to offer more convenience themselves. They might be tempted to develop their own delivery services. This could be risky; delivery might just add to their costs without a significant return in profit. Instead, the way to win back customers and keep existing customers was to coordinate with YourGrocer—a partner who would deliver groceries on their behalf. They didn't have to change their product at all.

Too often, businesses try to increase revenue by developing new products and features that are beyond their expertise. While they may capture more revenue, the endeavor ends up being a drain on time and money. This results in increased costs, minimal revenue gain, and likely a decrease in profits. Avoid this scenario by understanding why customers are switching away from your product. It could be that you can win back customers with little or no change to your product, as these small grocery stores did.

Create better advertising and promotional material by speaking to what customers value. Talk with customers to learn what messages connect with them. Don't simply show them a bunch of ads and ask what they like. Instead, learn what made them think that one solution was better than another. How did they describe using a product to their friends and family?

Morgan learned that just using the word quality didn't convey quality to customers. He needed to show pictures of the shops where the food came from. The shop logos did convey quality to customers.

Teams become more motivated, build consensus, and share a vision when they do Customer Jobs research together. Morgan's third cofounder, Frankie "Pragmatic," wanted to do JTBD research before joining YourGrocer. He also wanted to do it before he built anything. The benefits of this approach cannot be understated. First, the YourGrocer team immediately built consensus about what kind of product they needed to offer. Second, the team got the design of YourGrocer pretty spot-on the first time. They made a few adjustments along the way but never needed to make any significant pivots to the business model or how the company was going to solve its customers' JTBD.

7 THE FORCES OF PROGRESS

Forces that oppose each other
Unpacking demand generation
Push and pull shape the JTBD
Unpacking demand reduction
Put it to work

The last few case studies made frequent references to pushes, pulls, inertia, and anxieties. These four forces work together to generate and shape customer demand. This singular focus on customer motivation, and how forces shape customer demand, is what distinguishes JTBD from theories of innovation and design processes.

This chapter will introduce you to Customer Jobs thinking by unpacking the forces of progress. Understanding these forces will make you better at communicating customer motivation within your organization, understanding why customers are or are not attracted to your product, helping more customers buy your product, and creating advertising that connects with customers.

FORCES THAT OPPOSE EACH OTHER

The forces of progress are the emotional forces that generate and shape customers' demand for a product. They can be used to describe a high-level demand for any solution for the customers' JTBD or the demand for a specific product.

Two groups of forces work against each other to shape customer demand (figure 10). The first group is push and pull, or the forces that work together to generate demand. The other group is inertia and anxiety, or the forces that work together to reduce demand. In the middle, you have the customer, who experiences all these emotions at once.

Customers experience some combination of these forces before they buy a product, as they search for and choose a product, when they use a product, and when they use that product to make their lives better. Most innovators focus on the top two forces. They want to know "what customers want" and how demand is generated. They overlook the bottom two forces—that is, the forces that reduce and block that demand.

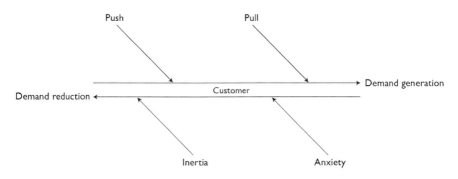

Figure 10. The forces of progress that create and reduce demand.

The innovators featured in this book are successful because they think about all four of these forces. Moreover, they think about how the forces contribute to the larger system that includes customers, producers, demand, and products. We'll study this larger system later in the book. For now, we'll unpack the four forces and understand how they generate and reduce demand.

UNPACKING DEMAND GENERATION

Demand isn't spontaneously generated. No one wakes up in the morning and suddenly thinks, *Today, I'm going to buy a new car.* Some combination of events always comes together to generate that demand. We call those forces push and pull.

Push. People won't change when they are happy with the way things are. Why would they? People change only when circumstances push them to be unhappy with the way things are. These pushes can be external or internal.

External pushes. Morgan learned that parents had no problem shopping at multiple food shops with one child. But when they had two or more children to haul around to all these food shops, you can imagine all the stress and effort involved in that (or you may have experienced it yourself). Each child has to be put into and taken out of a car seat, parents need to navigate shops with strollers and shopping carts, and they need to carry all their groceries back to their car with their children in tow. Finally, they have to do all this all over again at the next shop they visit.

Having a second child who makes grocery shopping unbearable is an example of a push. These parents have realized that their lives have changed, and the old way of solving their problems needs to change along with that.

Internal pushes. The Clarity and Form Theatricals case studies show examples of internal pushes. Clarity's customers were entrepreneurs who thought they were in a slump and struggled with motivation. Form Theatricals discovered various internal motivations that pushed customers to seek a solution for their struggle. These pushes ranged from frustration with the homogeneity of a peer group to parents who wanted experiences for their children that would teach life lessons.

In these examples, the outside world wasn't forcing customers to change. Rather, they experienced a combination of circumstances that made them think, I don't like how things are; I want to make a change.

Pull. If a push is the engine that powers customer motivation, the pull is the steering wheel that directs motivation. Customers experience two kinds of pulls: (1) an idea of a better life and (2) a preference for a particular product.

The pull for a better life. People don't buy products just to have or use them; they buy products to help make their lives better (i.e., make progress). When they have the right product for their problem, they are able to do things they couldn't before. The idea of this better life is what pulls them to act.

It's important to be able to answer the question "How will customers evolve when they have the right solution?" One way of thinking about this type of pull is to see what happens when customers don't recognize how life can be better (or refuse to act to improve it).

For example, Dan described how some entrepreneurs would sit in the dark and choose not to self-educate. It is important to note that these customers are aware of their desire to change but choose to do nothing about it.

People choose not to improve their lives for many reasons. Psychologist Gary Klein posits that customers must engage in various mental simulations before they take any kind of action. They need to make sense of their desire to evolve, and they need to create expectations of how life will be better when their struggle is resolved. A customer who fails to do either of those mental simulations will not be motivated to make a change.

For example, an entrepreneur who struggles with running her business might simply assume that such a struggle is an unavoidable aspect of entrepreneurship. She thinks, *that's just the way things are.* Another entrepreneur might recognize that the struggle is due to his inability to create a proper business model and assume that creating a business model is inherently hard.

The pull toward a solution. The pull for self-improvement is what motivates customers to begin searching for and using a solution. But what about their motivation to choose one solution over another? Dan learned that Clarity's customers thought about and evaluated solutions such as using LinkedIn, giving away adviser shares, and attending a conference. Why choose one over another?

There are many known and unknown factors to consider about why customers choose one solution over another. However, when we focus on the forces that generate demand, we see that the context of the customer's push shapes his or her desire to change. This affects the criteria used to choose one solution over another.

For example, attending a conference and using Clarity each compete for the same JTBD; however, one is not universally better than the other. If Clarity was universally better than attending a conference, then no one would attend conferences.

The reason that many options coexist is that the pushes that shape a desire for change contain many variations. Someone may want advice from successful entrepreneur Mark Cuban; however, that person may not be in a rush or may not even be sure exactly what his problem is. For these reasons, this person is willing to wait for the next time Mark Cuban speaks at a conference. Conversely, another entrepreneur might urgently need help with a specific problem that she knows Mark Cuban has solved and so is willing to pay a premium to have Cuban talk directly with her.

Variations in the pushes that customers experience also explain why the same customer might go back and forth between different products for the same JTBD. Sometimes, Clarity might be better; sometimes, attending a conference might be better. It all depends on the context of the struggle.

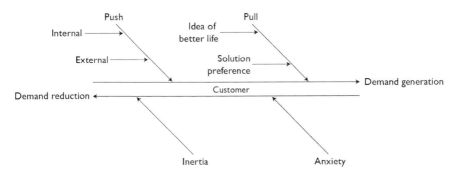

Figure 11. A breakdown of the forces that generate demand.

PUSH AND PULL SHAPE THE JTBD

There is no demand—and therefore no JTBD—unless push and pull work together. A powerful step in understanding customer motivation is to study and appreciate the interdependencies between push and pull. They need each other. I might be attracted to the idea of owning an electric car from Tesla, but I won't buy one unless I need a car. I have no push. Likewise, unless an electric car comes along that is attractive to me—it generates pull—I will accept that owning a car with an internal combustion engine is "just the way things are."

Generating demand. Appreciating the interdependency between push and pull is why Elon Musk decided that Tesla's first electric car would be a premium, high-end model. Musk believed he needed first to persuade customers that an electric car could be attractive, perform well, and be practical. He knew he needed to create pull to begin changing people's minds. Once he did that, he could begin producing less expensive cars with the manufacturing know-how gained through production experience while maintaining the company with the profits from selling high-margin cars. How's it working out? In 2016, about thirteen years after the company started, Tesla introduced its first low-end electric car. In the first week, it received an unprecedented 325,000 preorders for a car that customers had neither driven nor seen in person.[25]

Failing to generate demand. When you fail to appreciate the forces of progress generation and the interdependencies between them, you get an innovation like the Tata Nano. In 2008, Tata Motors believed it could offer a low-end, feature-minimal car that would shake up the automobile market. Various Harvard professors wrote books and case studies about its success, claiming that it was "a runaway best seller," a "disruptive innovation," and that it "may disrupt the entire automobile distribution system in India."[26]

However, the reality proved quite different. Nano sales have been abysmal. After six years of production, annual sales in 2015 were only 18,531. In the end, Tata spent $400 million developing a flop. The blunder has forced Tata Motors to lay off workers and engage in costly redesigns.[27]

Why did the Nano fail? It didn't have enough pull. In its cost-cutting frenzy, Tata didn't offer a stereo and air-conditioning—features that customers expected from a car. Poor design made it roll over easily and prone to fire, and its weak engine made it underpowered for mountain driving. As a result, many customers decided to stick with their motorcycles or to spend the same amount of money on a used car that offered more features.[28]

As of 2016, Tata has abandoned the idea of finding profit at the low end of the market. Instead, the company is trying to find profit by marching up market with the redesigned Nano GenX. The company is adding more pull to the Nano, so it competes with traditional cars from other manufacturers, such as Smart.[29]

If your product doesn't help customers make progress, price doesn't matter. Both Tesla and Tata understood the push(es) to own a car, but only Tesla appreciated the role pull played.

As you'll learn in a later chapter, it's naïve to assume that customers will buy a product just because it's a low-cost, feature-minimal version of an existing product. If that were true, netbooks would have displaced PCs and laptops, and everything inside the dollar store would be stealing away customers from the high-end products they copy.

My colleague Ryan D. Hatch once said, "High price may actually draw in customers rather than push them away. It implies quality." He's absolutely right. Lower price as a differentiator sounds nice in a PowerPoint presentation, in an MBA program, or on a spreadsheet, but innovators know better. They understand that customers value progress above everything else. What good is low price if the product cannot help you get the Job Done?

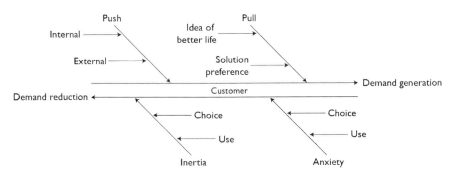

The Forces of Progress

Figure 12. All the forces, broken down.

UNPACKING DEMAND REDUCTION

Demand-reduction forces are just as important to understand as demand-generating forces. Most innovators and businesses focus on the latter and ignore the former. They shouldn't, though. Forces that reduce or block demand should be investigated and managed with the same enthusiasm as demand generation. Why? These forces are just as much competitors as any product produced by a competing business.

For example, a struggling customer may be willing to buy your product but doesn't because he fears that it's too hard to use. Instead, he sticks to an old way of doing things, even though he's unhappy with it. In this example, the result for you is the same, regardless of whether the customer stays with the current way of solving problems or buys a competitor's solution: you miss out on a paying customer.

Anxiety. In 2001, a collection of researchers lead by George Loewenstein identified two types of emotions that create anxiety: anticipatory emotions and anticipated emotions. The former are the feelings experienced only at the moment of decision, while the latter are what we expect to feel in the future. Within the context of JTBD and the forces of progress, I respectively call them anxiety-in-choice and anxiety-in-use.[30]

Anxiety-in-choice. We experience anxiety-in-choice when we don't know if a product can help us get a Job Done. It exists only when we've never used a particular product before. For example, "I've never taken the bus to work. Is it ever on time? Where do I buy a ticket?" We do our best to simulate mentally

91

how things will be when we match a particular solution with a JTBD. However, the more unknowns we face, the more worried we become. Some examples of anxiety-in-choice from our case studies include the following:

> If I use Clarity, will I sound stupid? Is the call going to be recorded? How is payment handled?

> This show seems interesting, but it got bad reviews. Maybe it's not worth getting tickets for.

> How does YourGrocer work? Are there flexible delivery options? Can I get my order today?

These anxiety-induced unknowns are associated with how—or if—a product can deliver progress. These are the anxieties that drive away first-time customers.

Anxiety-in-use. After customers use a product for a JTBD, the anxiety-in-choice largely disappears. Now their concerns are related to anxiety-in-use. For example, "I've taken the bus to work several times. But sometimes it's late, and other times it's early. I wish I knew its arrival time in advance." In this case, we know a product can deliver progress, but certain qualities about it make us nervous about using it.

Dan also discovered anxiety-in-use among his customers. He learned that customers wanted to use Clarity more but were held back because they were not sure how to prep for calls. They know a Clarity call can deliver them progress, but will they be satisfied with the next call? These are the anxieties that drive away repeat customers.

Inertia. Just as customers experience different types of anxieties, customers experience different types of inertia. Think of inertia as "a tendency to do nothing or to remain unchanged." Inertia can manifest in different ways. Mostly, inertia forces are habits: habits-in-choice and habits-in-use. Understanding customers' habits plays an important part in your ability to offer innovations.

Habits-in-choice. These are the forces that exist at the moment of decision and prevent a customer from switching from one product to another. My favorite example of this is how the spreadsheet software Excel finally overtook its competitor, Lotus 1-2-3. In the 1980s, Lotus 1-2-3 was the go-to choice for spreadsheet software. Then, Excel came on the scene. At first, many people wanted to use it. But because they already had all their data stored in Lotus 1-2-3 files, they couldn't switch. Microsoft solved this problem by giving Excel the ability to import and export Lotus 1-2-3 files. This eliminated the force that was holding customers back from switching to Excel.

Habits-in-use. When Morgan and his YourGrocer team started their research, they didn't explicitly search for problems around habit. But they quickly discovered a behavioral pattern: customers switched from using YourGrocer regularly to using it irregularly. This transition was an early indicator that a customer was about to fall out of the online-grocery buying cycle and switch back to shopping at the supermarket.

What was going on? Morgan learned that these disruptions in buying patterns were the consequences of a habit. Many customers had developed the habit of not planning for future grocery needs. They got it because they had been shopping at supermarkets—that is, their previous solution for their JTBD. Having a supermarket less than five minutes away meant that customers didn't need to plan their meals very much. They had gotten used to this and so formed a habit.

Morgan had discovered an instance where a habit-in-use reduced customer demand for his product. We know that these customers wanted to use YourGrocer because if they hadn't, they wouldn't have used it in the first place. However, old habits-in-use were blocking them from continuing to use YourGrocer. Over time, they would regress to using a previous solution. They regressed not because the other solution was better but because customers found that keeping their old habits was easier. If Morgan wanted to keep as many of his customers as possible, he needed to help them drop old habits-in-use and develop new ones.

Inertia and anxiety are your silent competitors. At its core, innovation is about helping customers make progress. Get them to that better version of life that they aspire to. It's not just about helping customers break constraints by pulling them with flashy, new features. A lot of not-so-sexy work is involved. YourGrocer is an example of these forces at work. If Morgan wanted to maintain his customers, he had to help them become better at planning their meals and grocery needs.

Samuel Hulick once told me that designing an innovation was similar to conducting an organ transplant. It's a wonderful analogy. The customer wants your product and hopes it will make life better, but for some reason, the switch doesn't happen. Customers get hung up on one little thing that blocks them from using your solution for their JTBD.

I ferociously attack inertia forces - like habit - as I would any competing product. I recommend you do the same. You can lose revenue because you haven't accounted for people's habits, or you can lose revenue because your product is inferior to a competing one. In both cases, the result is the same: you lose revenue.

Solving for customers' habits is often an easy win. Your prospective customer already knows about your product and wants to buy it but can't switch because of some small habit holding him or her back. All you have to do is figure out what's holding your customer back and solve it.

PUT IT TO WORK

First, study the push and pull. The easiest way to begin gathering data about the forces of progress is to identify pushes and pulls. These forces are largely experienced outside any product. You should check off these forces first and then dig into the exploration of any product. Push and pull help you understand how demand is generated and help you set some boundaries when exploring customer motivation.

> Find pushes by first asking about the solutions that customers have used. At what point did they realize that their particular solution wasn't working anymore? What was going on in their lives?

> Find pulls by asking about their opinions about other products they investigated. Why did they choose product X or product Y? What was wrong with product Y? What did X have that Y didn't?

Dig into inertia and anxiety after identifying push and pull. After you understand the forces that generate demand, study the demand-reducing forces. These arise when customer demand meets a product. They can also describe demand reduction for any given product.

For example, customers who hire attending a conference experience a different set of demand-reducing forces (i.e., inertia and anxieties) compared with if they choose Clarity. A customer who is shy may choose attending a conference because the idea of talking directly to an expert makes him or her nervous.

Fight anxiety and generate pull by helping customers visualize the progress they will make by using your product. Show them how their lives will be better. You could show customers how your company's outdoor grill is made of the latest and greatest advances in cooking technology. Or you could show customers how great of a cook they will become—and how their family and friends will be impressed—when they use your outdoor grill.

Earlier, we introduced the idea that customers engage in various mental processes: they make sense of their current problem, they try to envision how life will be better when they overcome that problem, and they simulate what it is like to use a product and its effect on their desire to evolve. This process takes a lot of work on the customers' part.[31]

Do customers a favor: help them visualize making progress. Create marketing and advertising materials that tell customers that you understand their struggle for progress, that help them visualize how life will be better when they have the right solution, and that explain why your product is the right solution.

Reduce anxiety-in-choice with trials, refunds, and discounts. "Buy one, get one free!" "Lifetime guarantee!" "Free shipping!" "Thirty-day refund!" These are probably the most obvious and widely practiced techniques of managing cost/value expectation. We're all familiar with them and have heard enough about discounts in Anthony's case study on theater tickets. We don't need to go into the subject further.

Identify any habits-in-use that keep customers from using your product. Adjust your product to help them along. Morgan learned that after using YourGrocer, many customers reverted to shopping at supermarkets, even though they preferred the food from YourGrocer. How did he help them? You'll remember that he created automated e-mail notifications encouraging customers to "reorder an entire box with one click" and asking, "Need anything? Get a free refill." The idea was to help these customers think ahead and make it easier for them to plan meals.

Comparing the habits of your best customers with the habits of those who recently quit is a great way to figure out how to turn switchers (i.e., those who have stopped using your product and started using another) into loyal customers. The first group have adapted and developed the necessary skills to get their Jobs Done (change their life-situation). Learn from them and use those data to help customers who are struggling get their Jobs Done.

8 WHEN YOU DEFINE COMPETITION WRONG

Too "kool" for school?
Why did the chotuKool flop?
The mainframe versus the PC
Don't be fooled by randomness
Put it to work

The forces of progress we spoke of earlier can help you understand how demand is generated and reduced. Creative destruction helps you understand the zero-sum nature of competition and how the definition of competition should not be restricted to products that look or function similarly.

But what happens when you ignore the forces of progress, creative destruction, and a constancy of purpose to solve a customer's JTBD? What happens when you insist on selling a particular type of product? What happens when you blindly apply a theory to innovation?

This chapter will answer those questions. With this knowledge, you can avoid the costly mistakes that others have made.

TOO "KOOL" FOR SCHOOL?

In 2006, Indian manufacturer Godrej believed it had found a vast, untapped market for household appliances: the hundreds of millions of low-income Indians. Could Godrej create a suitably affordable appliance? Godrej believed that it could succeed in a market that other companies overlooked.

But there were unanswered questions: Did an innovation opportunity really exist? What kind of product should the company create? How should it design the product? How would the product be sold? Godrej decided that it needed some help.

A Harvard professor's theory. Godrej hired economist and Harvard Business School professor Dr. Clayton Christensen and his consulting firm, Innosight. At Godrej's headquarters, Christensen presented some of his innovation theories to its management teams, and they discussed the market opportunity that millions of low-income Indians represented. Christensen agreed that it was a great opportunity, and he suggested that Godrej begin with a low-cost, feature-minimal refrigerator. It would be—as Christensen calls it—

Figure 13. The original chotuKool was positioned as a "disruptive innovation".

a "disruptive innovation." Godrej took Christensen's advice and hired his consulting firm to aid them in creating what would become the chotuKool.[32]

About a year later, in 2008, the chotuKool was publicly released to great fanfare. George Menezes, COO of Godrej Appliances, said, "In three years [we will sell] probably millions." It even won the Edison Award for Social Impact. Harvard and other business schools wrote case studies praising its innovation success and benefits to society. Dr. Christensen even created a video describing how the chotuKool would create "inclusive growth" that would improve India's economy and standards of living. Godrej exuberantly planned a platform of similar products, such as the chotuWash washing machine and a low-cost water purifier.[33]

However, reality was quite different. Using a test market of about 114.2 million people, Godrej had sold fifteen thousand units after two years. The chotuKool was an utter disaster. Godrej quietly abandoned plans for the chotuWash as well as any plans to create further "disruptive innovations."[34]

Redesign, reposition, and relaunch. Recognizing it was a flop, Godrej engaged in a costly redesign of the chotuKool. As of 2016, it's still being sold, but it's no longer targeted at low-income Indians. Instead, it's being advertised to middle-class Indians as a high-end, feature-rich portable cooler. Navroze Godrej, director of innovation and strategy, described the new chotuKool as "a

Figure 14. The chotuKool was repositioned to serve a mid-level buyer.

lifestyle product that people use in cars." G. Sunderraman, a Godrej vice president, commented on the repositioning: "How can you expect poor consumers with a minimum sustenance to be your pot of gold?" He also said, "We are now targeting a midlevel buyer."[35]

To add insult to injury, this new strategy is directly opposite from the one Godrej had started with. It had wanted a disruptive innovation that offered millions of Indians an inexpensive alternative to the household refrigerator, but the company now makes a luxury alternative to the inexpensive Styrofoam cooler.

WHY DID THE CHOTUKOOL FLOP?

Godrej made numerous mistakes leading up to the chotuKool. We can learn a lot about Customer Jobs and innovation when we compare and contrast its approach to a Customer Jobs approach.

Godrej began with a solution instead of a JTBD. The first thing Godrej and Christensen did was to consider which solution to make. Oddly, they came to the decision to create a refrigerator before talking with any potential customers. They jumped to this conclusion because they were following the theory of disruptive innovation, which restricts innovation efforts to a group of specific solutions and technologies. Godrej and Christensen assumed that consumers wanted a low-cost refrigerator, and that this would make the chotuKool successful.

Customer Jobs rejects solution-first approaches and rejects the idea that products of only the same type can be competitors. Customer Jobs argues that you must begin by understanding the customers' JTBD and how they see competition. Remember the forces of progress: what is pushing and pulling customers to make a change? Don't assume that customers will buy a particular product just because it's a cheaper version of another or that they are unhappy with whatever solution they are currently using for a JTBD.

Godrej followed its own prejudices and discounted customer motivation. The company did a great deal of research before it designed the chotuKool. Its research team visited people's homes, observed how they lived, and conducted interviews. Here are some excerpts from them:

> "I don't feel the need for a refrigerator. I use an earthen pot to cool water. I buy vegetables for immediate consumption and boil milk to avoid it from getting spoilt."

> "In India, a refrigerator costs around eight thousand to ten thousand rupees. In addition, it has a running expense, which will upset my monthly budget. I don't have the space to keep it in my tiny house."

> "To me, a refrigerator should cost around twenty-five hundred rupees, and running it should be affordable. How will I service it if needed? My neighbor had to shell out twenty-five hundred rupees for servicing it and an additional three hundred rupees to transport it to a service center. I face load-shedding of six to eight hours every day. How will the product work?"

Godrej actually got valuable information about customer motivation, but it seems that it chose to ignore the most important parts. Instead of digging deeper into "I don't feel the need for a refrigerator," it focused on "a refrigerator should cost around twenty-five hundred rupees and running it should be affordable."

Why did Godrej do this? Well, it had already decided to create a low-end refrigerator, so it listened to data that confirmed only its prejudices and ignored all the warning signs that consumers had little or no interest in any kind of electric refrigerator.[36]

What was the biggest mistake that Christensen and Godrej made? Christensen and Godrej created the chotuKool based on the theory of disruptive innovation. This theory has critical flaws. The biggest? It relies on an oversimplified model of competition that does not take into account how customers see competition. In this case, the theory limits the competition for electric refrigerators to only other electric refrigerators. This is why Christensen and Godrej completely misunderstood the competitive landscape. They did not consider Schumpeter's warning that competition should not be restricted to products of the same type. Competition can come from anywhere.

Customer Jobs invalidates many theories—like disruptive innovation—that try to model and predict the dynamics of a market. Here are a few reasons why:

> They oversimplify the competitive landscape. JTBD shows us that competition can rarely be restricted to just one type of technology or innovation. Think about all the different types of innovations that compete with Clarity, theater, or YourGrocer.

> These theories don't take into consideration that customers often combine multiple products together to form one solution for a JTBD. This is something we'll see shortly.

> They don't take into consideration how customers view competition. People who create these models rarely, if ever, talk with customers and learn how they see competition. A competitive model that doesn't come from customers will be invalid. The chotuKool is such an example.

> These theories assume that the competitive landscape won't change in the future. Competition for a product changes continually. Moreover, often what renders an innovation obsolete isn't a cheaper or simpler version of itself; rather, it's when the system around an innovation changes so much that it doesn't fit anymore. Apple's iPod wasn't made obsolete by another type of MP3 player; it was made obsolete by an app on a smartphone. While the fuel injector made the carburetor obsolete, what will make the fuel injector obsolete won't be a new way of mixing gas and air—it will be electric cars that don't even use engines or gas!

When we acknowledge the complex nature of competition for a JTBD, we can see why rural Indians in Godrej's target market saw competition to an electric refrigerator as follows:

> Buying vegetables every day for immediate consumption.

> Boiling milk to prevent it from spoiling.

> Keeping water in clay pots at home.

> Using a more than three-thousand-year-old innovation called a pot-in-pot to keep food and water cold.

> Using other clay-based cooling innovations, such as the MittiCool.

Godrej's own research had revealed that customers were already hiring these solutions for their JTBD. However, because Godrej had a bias to follow the theory of disruptive innovation, the company chose to ignore these data.

Godrej believed in an idea called "nonconsumption" or "nonusers." Navroze Godrej describes how "Clayton and the Innosight team were insistent on focusing on nonusers." In other words, the company was led to believe these Indians lacked the money or skill to buy and use any product for their JTBD. That's what Christensen and his team meant by "nonusers" or that "nonconsumption" was taking place. What do you think? Would you consider these Indians as nonconsumers or nonusers? Unfortunately for Godrej, the company learned the answer to this question the hard way: these Indians were consumers, but they just weren't consumers of electric refrigerators.[37]

JTBD rejects the idea of nonusers or nonconsumption. Just because consumers aren't using your product, or another product of the same type, doesn't mean they are nonusers. This is another big difference between JTBD and other approaches to markets and innovation. JTBD insists that if consumers have a JTBD, they must be using something for it.

Here's the twist: That "something" that consumers use for their JTBD doesn't include products that one can only buy. It includes any compensatory behavior, paying someone else for help, making one's own solution, or combining solutions. Each counts as a solution for a JTBD.

We actually heard about this in Godrej's own research. One interviewee claimed that she would "buy vegetables for immediate consumption and boil milk to avoid it from getting spoilt." Combined, those two actions count as a solution for a JTBD. In the customer's mind, they are competition to the chotuKool.

If Godrej wanted consumers to buy a chotuKool, Godrej needed to offer its target buyers a solution that would persuade them to give up the solutions they were currently hiring for their JTBD. Sadly, the people leading this project didn't think about that.

Godrej didn't understand that the chotuKool had little to no profit potential. The company assessed chotuKool's potential by applying the theory of disruptive innovation. Instead, it should have applied some simple math. If it had, any plans to create the chotuKool would have been immediately abandoned. Unfortunately, it took the failure of the chotuKool for Godrej to realize that it had been a mistake to create any type of "low-end" innovation for low-income consumers. Recall what Godrej vice president G. Sunderraman said: "How can you expect poor consumers with a minimum sustenance to be your pot of gold?"

The chotuKool was never going to make much money targeting low-income Indians. Why? In our discussion of creative destruction and profits, we pointed out that competition is a zero-sum game. Profits have to come from somewhere. Whose profits was the chotuKool going to steal? Its target customers were people who lived on only a few dollars a day. How were they going to afford a sixty-dollar to seventy-dollar chotuKool? This price point would have made sense if consumers were spending that kind of money on comparable solutions. Or perhaps they would consider saving up their money if the chotuKool improved their lives dramatically. Neither of these conditions, however, were remotely true. Again, think about the forces of progress. It would have taken a great deal of push and pull to persuade customers to switch from using a free solution for their JTBD to using one they have to pay for. For these consumers, using a clay pot and buying vegetables daily was a good-enough solution for their JTBD.

THE MAINFRAME VERSUS THE PC

Innovation is hard and unpredictable. I've had my share of innovation mishaps. And admittedly, if I had been in Godrej's place, I might have made some of the same mistakes. It's easy to stand on the sidelines and critique what someone else does wrong. But there are two mistakes I sure as heck wouldn't have made:

> Limiting my definition of competition to products that look and function similarly.

> Not making sure a true desire for change was taking place and that customers were willing—and able—to pay for a solution.

These are common mistakes when you don't apply a JTBD view to competition. But they aren't the only ones.

A less common mistake—but just as dangerous—is to believe that products are competitors when they are not. One example of this is the widespread belief that PCs and mainframes are (or were) competitors. Was that ever true? Were or are PCs just a cheaper, simpler version of mainframes? Did the introduction of PCs have any effect on the market for mainframes? Did the PC create a new market or tap into existing ones?

Understanding the story behind the PC versus the mainframe will help you learn how to think about competition, become better at identifying real threats to your business, create better messaging that properly speaks to what customers consider as competition, and know how you should and shouldn't design a solution.

Here's the common narrative about PCs versus mainframes. Mainframe computers are large hardware devices that have been used since the mid-twentieth century for massive calculations. Businesses and universities have used them for tasks such as accounting, payroll, and processing scientific data. Governments have used them for tasks such as processing census, tax, and military data (e.g., predicting the effects of atomic bombs).

Companies such as IBM sold to these customers, which were the only ones who could afford mainframes and had the skills to operate them. For many years, mainframes were very profitable. To continue grabbing as much profit as possible, makers produced more complicated machines that therefore sold at ever-increasing margins.

Then, in the late 1970s and early 1980s, PCs appeared. They were nowhere nearly as powerful as mainframes, but they did appeal to customers who couldn't afford a mainframe or didn't need so much computing power. PCs created a new market by appealing to these less demanding customers. Mainframe manufacturers were happy to give up the low-end market because the margins in it were so small.

Unfortunately for the mainframe manufacturers, however, the PC got better and better. Eventually, they were just as good, if not better, than mainframes for doing many computational tasks. As a result, the PC created a huge new market and ultimately eliminated the existing mainframe industry.[38]

The innovator's—false—dilemma. That's certainly an interesting story. Yet it's totally wrong.

Before we apply a JTBD perspective here, let's consider some numbers. Here's what Toni Sacconaghi of Bernstein Research recently said about IBM:

> The mainframe is a hugely profitable business for IBM. Only around 4 percent of the firm's revenues come from mainframe sales. But once additional hardware, storage, software, and all kinds of related services have been factored in, the mainframe accounts for a quarter of IBM's revenue and nearly half of profits.[39]

It seems that the mainframe business is alive and kicking. In fact, in 2012, IBM announced the newest addition to its line of mainframe computers: the z12. It cost $1 billion to develop and had a starting price of around $1 million. The plan worked well: today, approximately 96 percent of the world's top one hundred banks, 92 percent of the twenty-five top US retailers, and nine of ten of the world's largest insurance companies run IBM's System z mainframes. In 2013, IBM's revenue was $99.8 billion. Building on the z12's success, it launched the z13 in 2015. So, what's going on? The PC had supposedly disrupted the mainframe business. Let's put a JTBD lens on this story and see what we can find.[40]

To make sense of it all, we need to ask again if mainframes and PCs were ever in competition with each other. And if you recall, if we want to get an accurate model of competition for JTBD, we have to understand how customers see competition. So, let's take a look at who buys PCs and mainframes, what they are used for, and what each replaced.

Why mainframes? Mainframes have always provided a level and type of computing power that has appealed only to a few. They were first used for intensive mathematical calculations, such as predicting the effects of the first

Figure 15. Creative destruction in action. A mainframe replaced scores of "computers," the machines they worked on, and the people who supervised them (top). A 1953 picture of "computers" from what would become nasa's jet propulsion lab (bottom).

atomic bomb and processing census data. For scientific or government computations, the alternative was to hire scores of mathematicians (who were usually women in the first decades of computing; they themselves were referred to as "computers") to do the calculations by hand. For businesses, the alternative to a mainframe was scores of secretaries and clerks who either did payroll and sales data by hand or operated cumbersome, electromechanical calculating machines such as the Friden Electro-Mechanical Calculator.[41]

Today, many of the same entities use mainframes for tasks similar to those of sixty years ago. In fact, today, they are used in an ever-increasing number of contexts. A mainframe most likely processes ATM transactions at any major

106

bank. Global logistics firms such as DHL run mainframe systems to support their core business processes.[42]

The progress that mainframes deliver today is incredibly similar to what they delivered sixty years ago—namely, the confidence that comes with having a computing competitive advantage and the peace of mind that you can securely run mission-critical processes.

Are PCs competition for mainframes? Here are the real questions: Did purchases of PCs have any impact on the sales of mainframes? Did mainframe manufacturers miss out on a budding market? Is there any relationship between the two types of computer at all?

Today, it is safe to say that there is no competitive relationship between PCs and mainframes. Does anyone ever think, Hmm, do I buy a mainframe, or do I buy a PC? Has a company ever replaced a mainframe with a PC? Of course not. Remember, you can claim that two products are competitors only if you can find a customer who has switched from one to the other.

But what about PCs versus mainframes thirty years ago—when PCs first became popular? Well, in 1984, PC Magazine interviewed Dr. Norm Agin of Martin Marietta Data Systems about the company's recent PC purchases. When asked about PCs replacing mainframes, Agin "scoffs at the notion that putting in PCs reduces the load on the company mainframe." Agin said, "We picked IBM PCs for compatibility with [our existing IBM] mainframes" and that employees using a PC represented a switch from "having a calculator and typewriter on [their] desk."

Agin's comments begs important questions such as: (1) How can PCs and mainframes be competitors if customers use them together? (2) Are these PCs competing with costly mainframes or cheap calculators and typewriters?[43]

Agin dismissing the competitive relationship between mainframes and PCs is far from unique. We can get a good idea of how consumers in the 1970s and 1980s saw PCs by turning to YouTube's nearly endless supply of old PC commercials:[44]

> IBM's 5100 PC, released in 1977, promises to help real estate investors "manage all the difficult decisions." Avionic designers could "save time and money" by calculating flight expenses in the office.

A 1980 ad has actor William Shatner ask viewers, "Why just buy a video game from Atari? Invest in the wonder computer of the 1980s: the Commodore Vic-20." You can even play "Gorf, the wonder arcade game" with your new Commodore.

The Apple IIe promises to "teach your children well" and helps baseball managers "manage player stats." The Apple IIc is also featured as an alternative to the IBM PC Junior.

The Tandy 1000, released in 1984, would remove all the clutter from your desk by "changing the way you work" with "DeskMate software for easy-to-use word processing, filing, worksheets, scheduling, and communications."

One thing is clear while watching these TV ads: not once is anyone making any reference whatsoever to mainframes. Moreover, these commercials don't make any mention of the high-throughput, transactional integrity tasks for which mainframes are used. Instead, we see PCs helping individuals and small businesses become more productive. Even I remember my first PC. It didn't replace a mainframe; it replaced my (less expensive and simpler to use) Atari game system. In the minds of customers, PCs and mainframes have no association whatsoever.

What was the PC's competition? Did PCs create a new market? These old TV commercials also make it perfectly clear that the competition for PCs was—and still is, in some cases—typewriters, word-processing machines, personal assistants, calculators, files and file cabinets, interoffice messaging services, graphic design and layout by hand, accounting services or accounting by hand, game systems (e.g., Atari), and tabletop games (e.g., Dungeons & Dragons).

The above alternatives represent solutions whose growth and profits were disrupted by PCs. Think back to our lessons from Schumpeter, competition, and creative destruction. When people began buying and using PCs, what did they stop buying and using? It wasn't mainframes. They stopped buying and using the various solutions above.

In addition, the invention of the PC represented a new market if you define markets only by products that look or function similarly. However, from a JTBD point of view, PCs didn't create a new market. Rather, PCs simply added an alternative to the existing markets that the solutions above constituted.

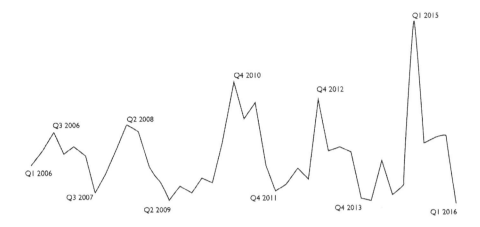

Figure 16. Changes in revenue from sales of IBM's mainframes. Dramatic drops and subsequent peaks in revenue are due to product introductions and customer buying patterns, not from customers switching to a competitor.

Was the PC really cheaper and simpler? The other point to notice is that the PC didn't necessarily represent a cheaper alternative to the solutions it replaced. This invalidates the idea that the PC was any kind of low-end, "disruptive" product. If you had an accounting firm, you could give one of your accountants a PC, and she would be able to do the work of ten accountants. That is certainly cheaper. However, a PC is neither simpler nor cheaper than a board game, a typewriter, or an Atari game system.

What do mainframes compete against today? Fifty years ago, mainframes competed against hiring scores of mathematicians and clerks, but what do mainframes compete against today? Once again, we have to find evidence of a switch if we want to answer that question. Luckily, such an example comes from Johnson & Johnson (J&J)—an American company that makes medical devices, pharmaceuticals, and consumer packaged goods (CPGs).

In 2015, J&J shut down its last mainframe. In place of owning mainframes, it switched to using a combination of cloud services from Amazon.com Inc., Microsoft Corp., and NTT Communications Corp. Stuart McGuigan, J&J's chief information officer, commented about the switch: "[It was not] something I was sure I'd see in my lifetime: A Fortune 100 company with absolutely no mainframe footprint." Why did they switch? J&J needed more computing power and using cloud services allows J&J to lower its infrastructure costs. In other words, J&J wanted more for less.[45]

What are the reasons for the mistaken correlation? So, why have people made this mistaken correlation between mainframes and PCs? I can think of two big reasons.

>   Correlation in physical appearance. If you don't know anything about mainframes or PCs, you'd be tempted to think the latter is simply a smaller version of the former and that they belong to the same market. Just because they are both computers doesn't mean they are used for the same Jobs.
>
>   A misunderstanding of how variation works. Because mainframes are very expensive, customers don't buy them often. This means mainframes have a sales cycle that can last a decade or more. If you were to focus on sales of mainframes in the middle of their sales cycle, you might think that demand had utterly vanished.

People who believe that PCs disrupted mainframe sales are making two common statistical errors. First, they mistake common-cause variation for special-cause variation—something discussed in chapter 19. There was no special decline in mainframe sales in response to the availability of PCs. Rather, mainframes have a very up-and-down sales cycle that is normal for them (figure 16). Second, such people conflate correlation and causation. Just because PC sales were going up at a time when mainframe sales were going down doesn't mean one caused the other.

To this day, IBM continues to make a tremendous amount of money selling both mainframes and supporting services. In 2014, IBM had revenue of $92.8 billion, with $21 billon in operating pretax income. The company has been around for more than one hundred years. It maintains success by continually producing high-margin products for customers who have an insatiable demand for more features and more quality.[46]

Finally, real competition to mainframes has only recently emerged in the form of cloud computing. From the customers' point of view, competition for the mainframe isn't owning any kind of computer but outsourcing everything to someone else.

DON'T BE FOOLED BY RANDOMNESS

You will become a better innovator when you recognize that innovation is hard, there are no recipes for success, and there's no "one right way" to make products and build businesses. It's why Steve Blank says, "No business plan survives first contact with customers." Why is this so? Because life is full of unknown and unknowable variation. Just because a product or business strategy worked once doesn't mean it work will again.

Unfortunately, that doesn't stop people from trying to sell you recipes for success. The early twentieth century saw Frederick Winslow Taylor sell "scientific management." Over the last thirty years, countless consultants and academics—who have never innovated themselves—have presumed to tell innovators about the right and wrong ways to innovate. Examples include *In Search of Excellence, Built to Last, Good to Great*, and *The Innovator's Dilemma*.[47]

However, history shows that such recipes for innovation and business success fail to live up to their promises. Here are some criticisms of these management and innovation theories, as well as their overall approach to research:[48]

> *The Halo Effect* by Phil Rosenzweig criticizes such formulas and theories as pseudoscientific and falling victim to what he called the "nine delusions"—for example, picking a successful company and making attributions about its culture, leadership, values without offering any objective, experimental data to support it.

> *Thinking, Fast and Slow* by Nobel Prize–winning psychologist Dr. Kahneman explains that we're drawn to these theories because they are done through entertaining storytelling that is "simple," "concrete rather than abstract," and "focus on a few striking events" instead of the myriad, smaller events that did or didn't happen.

> Bongo-playing, Nobel Prize–winning physicist Richard Feynman gave warning of what he called "cargo cult science" and decried these people as selling "science that isn't science." He pointed out that too often, people who are good storytellers can fool those of us who aren't experienced in scientific rigor or statistics. However, many of us who do have these skills recognize that these management and innovation gurus fall victim to what is

called "selecting the dependent variable." For example, suppose I have a theory that wearing red shorts causes shark attacks. To "prove" this theory, I research shark attacks that happen where the victim wore red shorts. Every time I find an instance where that happens, I pat myself on the back and tell everyone how smart I am. However, such an approach ignores instances where someone wore red shorts and was not attacked by a shark. Such data would invalidate my theory; however, I never find them because I never look for them.

Innovation and entrepreneurship is hard, full of self-doubt, and riddles us with anxiety about the future. I know; I've been there. Nevertheless, when we do find ourselves struggling, we must do our best to not be taken advantage of by these recipe peddlers and modern-day fortune tellers—no matter how confidently they claim to understand the behavior of markets or where their MBAs come from. If I can't convince you of the heavy costs these people exact on our economies, perhaps disaster stories such as the chotuKool and the $400-million flop of Tata's Nano can.

Customer Jobs frees us from recipe peddlers. Customer Jobs excites me because it doesn't try to sell me any plug-in-and-play plan for success. It respects the fact that innovation will always require critical thinking and hard work. That's what makes its message fundamentally different from what recipe peddlers sell. Customer Jobs doesn't tell me what kind of innovation I should make or how to build it. Instead, its restricts itself to (1) what customers are struggling with, (2) how they imagine their life being better when they have the right solution, and (3) what they do and don't value in a solution. Such an approach helps innovators like me find innovation opportunities and to navigate a world that is filled with the unknown and unknowable. I find this knowledge empowering. It's also why I've applied it to my own businesses and products. I believe it will help you become a better innovator as well.

PUT IT TO WORK

This chapter is a cautionary tale of what can happen when the principles of Customer Jobs are ignored or unknown. Here are a few things you can do to help you avoid making the same mistakes.

Don't restrict competition to products with similar functionality or physical characteristics. Don't assume two products are competitors because they look or function similarly. There are two related mistakes people make about what is and isn't competition for a product.

Thinking that two solutions compete against each other because they share similar characteristics. Even though PCs and mainframes are both computers, they don't compete in the slightest.

Restricting the definition of competition to products with similar characteristics. Godrej and Christensen believed that the only competition for their electric refrigerator was other electric refrigerators. They also believed they were creating a new market of refrigerator alternatives. Unfortunately for Godrej, neither of those opinions was true. Consumers were already using several refrigerator alternatives.

Keep your mind open to what counts as competition. I recently talked with a woman who told me about switching from her morning coffee to a kale smoothie with a shot of wheatgrass. Who would've thought a cup of coffee and a kale smoothie could be competitors?

Every innovator, whether creating a new innovation or improving an existing one, should have a clear idea of how his or her customers see competition. When you're creating a new innovation, you need to answer the question, "What are customers going to stop buying when they start buying our solution?" And if you're creating a new feature for an existing product, you need to ask, "What behaviors or other products is this feature going to replace?"

Talk with your customers! Your competitive model can come only from them. Models of competition and markets that don't come from customers are almost guaranteed to be wrong.

Don't study the relationships among customers, products, and competition just from afar. You must actually talk with the customers who use these products. Ask them what else they've tried to get the Job Done. Were there other options they wanted to try but didn't or couldn't? Did they combine solutions because no single solution worked well? Through questions like these, you can triangulate what customers do or don't consider as competition.

Confirm that competition exists between products by finding customers who switched. At the time of this writing, PC sales have dropped to historic lows; they've been on a decline for quite some time. Some people claim that this drop in PC sales is due to the smartphone. But is that true?[49]

Remember, correlation does not equal causation. There's only one sure way to prove a causal link between smartphone sales and PC sales: find people who stopped using their PCs and started using smartphones. Unless you can find evidence of a switch, the suggestion that any competitive relationship exists between the two is pure conjecture. Yes, some people may have entirely stopped using a PC in favor of a smartphone, but a lot of people own and use both. How would you interpret that?

Do you think you're creating a new market? Think again. For too long, businesses have created, and been encouraged to create, their own definitions of markets—that is, which products do and do not compete against each other. JTBD offers us a way to rethink how we define markets.

If you think you're creating a new market, then you probably haven't done enough research. Have you explored all the options that customers consider as competition for a JTBD solution? Perhaps customers are solving their problems in ways that don't require the purchase of a physical product. For example, a lot of people in New York City don't own a laundry machine. Instead, they drop off their laundry at laundromats for other people to clean and fold.

Another consideration is how customers often use a combination of solutions for a JTBD—for example, combining (1) boiling milk to make it last, (2) using a pot-in-pot, and (3) buying highly perishable foods only when they can be eaten right away.

If you don't have a clear picture of what customers are going to give up when they start using your product, either you haven't done enough research, or no JTBD exists and you're creating a solution that no one will buy.

Know what budget you're taking away from. When commenting on the chotuKool's initial failure, Godrej vice president G. Sunderraman said that "poor consumers with a minimum sustenance" were probably not a "pot of gold." He was absolutely correct. The chotuKool had been conceived without a clear picture of what budget it was going to take from.

Dan Martell avoided this problem because he did acquire a clear picture. He knew that Clarity was taking money away from budgets for attending conferences, paying for LinkedIn, hiring consultants, and giving away advisory shares.

Having a clear picture of what budget you're going take money away from helps you figure out what the revenue potential for an innovation is—if there's any at all—and how much money to invest in creating and selling an innovation.

Continually refresh the competitive landscape with ongoing feedback from customers. What customers count as competition for a JTBD is always changing. Don't assume that it remains static. Somewhere, unknown to you, your customers might have come across a new way of getting the Job Done. This is why you need to interact with your customers continually.

Your best bet is to talk with your customers regularly and keep interviewing new ones. Learn the stories behind their purchases. What solutions have they tried? What other solutions did they consider before buying yours? For existing customers, learn if they've heard about or tried other solutions. For customers who've stopped using your product, ask them why. Have they switched to a new solution, or does the JTBD no longer exist for them?

Remember that not every JTBD needs to be solved with a product that customers buy. Perhaps the most common reason that an innovation fails is that no one wants it. A great many innovators and entrepreneurs get excited about solving people's problems. This is a good thing. The downside is that most consumers are fine with good-enough solutions for a JTBD, and many of those don't require a purchase. As Des Traynor, cofounder of Intercom, says, "The popularity of product-first businesses has led to short-sightedness around what's necessary to create a sustainable business. Some problems persist because they're quite simply not worth solving."[50]

The chotuKool case study offers many perfect examples of customers who had good-enough solutions for a JTBD. Rural Indians might like the idea of a small refrigerator, but they were fine using clay pots and shopping for food every day. The chotuKool was a luxury item that didn't deliver much more progress than their current solutions.

PART III

THE SYSTEM OF PROGRESS

As I've noted, a study of a customer's JTBD is fundamentally a study of a system. We are interested in how the system's parts work together to help customers make progress.

In our next case study, we'll see how Omer Yariv was able to discover a JTBD and create a product for it by focusing on the energy behind customers' struggling moments. Justin Jackson's and Ash Maurya's case studies will help you understand better what "customers want progress" and "a JTBD is part of a system" mean. Finally, we'll look at the system of progress and how the study of it helps create sustainable businesses that make products that customers will buy.

9 CASE STUDY: OMER AND TRANSCENDENT ENDEAVORS

What's the JTBD?
Put it to work

I met Omer Yariv at the Customer Jobs Meetup I run here in New York City. At the time, he was vice president of engineering and product at a start-up called Simplist—its product helps you search for specific people within your social network. I particularly enjoy talking with Omer. We share a background in writing, engineering, and, of course, Customer Jobs.

Omer joined Transcendent Endeavors (TE) in 2014 and is senior product manager now. Many of TE's products are about facilitating communication between nurses, doctors, and patients. Omer is in charge of a new-product initiative for helping hospitals improve patient care. He shared with me how he's using Customer Jobs principles to create a product from scratch.

Omer knew which customers he needed to talk with, how to unpack their desire to evolve, and how to figure out what kind of solution would or wouldn't help them make progress.

How Customer Jobs helped Omer get started. Omer's first task at TE was to develop a solution to prevent adverse events at hospitals—that is, circumstances in which someone's condition declines because of something other than what brought him or her in for care. Examples are falls, infections, and bedsores.

When he started, Omer didn't know very much about the health-care industry, but that didn't concern him much. He was confident that he could create a successful product; all he had to do was find a group of people who were struggling to get a Job Done. Who struggled the most with adverse events? He looked for answers. Who had the most to lose when adverse events happened? Who had the most to gain by preventing them? Who was putting the most energy—the most effort—into finding a solution that helped prevent adverse events? Omer believes that finding this energy is imperative to discovering a JTBD:

> When I interview potential customers, I look for evidence of a struggle. I'm looking for an energy to tap into. That's how I know

a struggling moment exists and that there's an opportunity to create something. If a group of people is not struggling—if I can't feel that energy—then there's probably no opportunity there.

How does Customer Jobs help you create a product that people actually want to use? At this point, Omer didn't have very much to go on. All he knew was that adverse events happen at hospitals and that nobody wants them to happen. He said,

> Hospitals don't want adverse events. It costs them money. It costs them time. It costs them reputation. Patients don't want adverse events. Who wants to get sicker? Nurses don't want adverse events because they're there to take care of patients. Nobody in the system wants adverse events to happen. How come they still happen? Where's the gap there? What's missing?

Omer was wrestling with a tough question. Why do adverse events happen, even though so many people don't want them to? The fact that so many people were affected by adverse events made it hard to know where to start. Omer knew he couldn't build a solution for everyone. Not only would it be expensive and difficult, but there was no guarantee that all the people would actually use it.

Omer's experience as an innovator had taught him an important lesson: many products fail simply because no one wants them. Of course, he wanted to make something people would actually use. He narrowed his focus on one group of people who struggled the most (who suffered the greatest consequences at any adverse event) and those who were in a position to prevent adverse events.

How do you figure out who struggles the most? Omer needed to find out who had the most emotional motivation to prevent adverse events, for they would most likely use whatever product he created. He began by casting a wide net:

> I wanted to interview potential users [those who will use it] and potential customers [those who will pay for it]. But I had to find the right ones to interview. I wanted to talk with those who had the most energy—who had the most motivation to solve the problem. So, I started creating surveys for the different people involved in adverse events, such as nurses and medical office managers.

Omer asked such employees how long they had worked in the field, how often they saw (and managed) adverse events, and whether they thought adverse events were preventable. He began to see who might be best to interview in more depth:

> We learned that we needed to talk with nurses who had a lot of patients—and who had to deal with high turnover of those patients. These two conditions ruled out intensive care units [ICUs] and oncology [cancer treatment]. In ICUs, you have only one or two patients to watch over. There is also a high turnover of those patients. You're dealing with a limited number of patients, and you're not in charge of them for very long. In oncology, you might have ten patients, but you work with them over a long period of time. You get to know them. But with nurses involved in med/surg [medical/surgical], there seemed to be an opportunity there.

Nurses in medical/surgical face a different challenge compared with other nurses. Medical/surgical nurses watch over at least four or five patients at a time, and these turn over within a few days. It's a tough situation; patients constantly come and go. Nurses learn about their patients' conditions and needs and care for them for a few days. But just as nurses get to know patients better, new patients take their place. These working conditions are why nurses in medical/surgical deal with the most adverse events. Omer concluded that medical/surgical nurses desired the most change and would be the most likely to use whatever product his team ended up creating.

Omer's next step was to dive into the struggle this particular group of nurses faced. In interviews, he would ask what the struggle was like. Were the nurses trying to prevent adverse events? If so, how?

Discover a customer's JTBD through an interview by looking for the energy of a desire to evolve. Learn how the customer wants life to be. Omer's first interviews asked broad questions:

> Does your hospital talk about adverse events?

> Are there incentives if the number of adverse events goes up or down?

How would you describe your daily life as a nurse? What are your routines?

What is it like when adverse events happen on your watch?

But grabbing just any old data from interviews can make things worse instead of better. To avoid that, Omer looked for signs that these nurses were struggling to make progress:

> All through those questions, I'm always looking for energy. If they describe their struggle using a particular solution, or if they describe having any emotional motivation to make things better, I would know that I needed to dig into it more. I was always looking for energy.

Omer kept looking for "energy" around a desire for change. Was there any change in body language or how the nurses talked while describing dealing with adverse events? Did some express frustration with procedures or products they used that left them feeling powerless? What was giving them the most anxiety and stress? What were the forces of progress (i.e., push, pull, anxiety, and inertia)? Sure enough, Omer's persistent search for energy paid off:

> I finally started to get an idea of the struggle they faced as a nurse— and in particular when dealing with adverse events. For example, I had no idea that nurses don't always get along; they don't always like one another. The situation the hospital puts them in leads them to feel that they're alone against everybody.

The "situation" Omer refers to is how hospitals decide who is liable when an adverse event happens. Nurses generally suffer any consequences, even when an event is not their fault. For example, if a doctor prescribes the wrong medication and the nurse administers it, the nurse is liable, although he or she was not the source of the problem. Such an adverse event goes on a nurse's permanent record, and he or she could lose a job, lose a license, or be sued. All this can happen because of someone else's mistake. If all that stress isn't enough, there's the social stigma that nurses can face when an adverse event happens on their watch. Omer said,

> There's a very strong feeling of 'I don't want to be that nurse that all the other nurses are talking about.' That's another very big

motivation to make a change. All these struggles create a lot of energy to change things for the better. It's a JTBD.

You found a struggle for progress. Now what? Learn how customers imagine their lives being better. Omer had found a struggle: nurses were afraid of being held liable for adverse events happening on their watch. But he wanted to learn more. How did these nurses want things to be? What would their lives be like if this struggle were resolved? He said,

> Even with all this struggle they face, you kind of wonder, why do they want to be a nurse? The answer they gave was always the same: They're there because they feel like they can make a change. They feel like they're helping people. That's the thing that keeps them going—the feeling that you're helping someone.

> These nurses want to help people, and that's why they became nurses in the first place. This was an important piece of their JTBD puzzle.

Armed with these two insights— (1) the struggle and consequences nurses face regarding adverse events and (2) nurses' desire to feel as if they are helping other people—Omer now had a pretty good idea of what Job these customers were struggling with and what their lives would be like when it got Done.

Omer now needed to learn what these nurses valued in a solution. This would help guide his team in designing one to fit the JTBD.

How do you learn what customers want in a solution for a JTBD? Even though Omer had a pretty good idea of these nurses' JTBD, he didn't know what they would expect in a solution. A JTBD describes the customer's problem and only hints at what a solution should be. Omer needed to learn the following:

How nurses currently handled adverse events.

What solutions they had tried.

What they did and didn't value in each solution.

Whether they were expressing compensatory behaviors.

Whether they were using a combination of solutions because no single solution was good enough.

The answers proved fruitful:

> The story here is that nurses have a lot of things to remember. They want to get them right. There's a lot at stake if a mistake is made. Nurses take care of people, they run around, they get interrupted, and then they have to put everything into the documentation later.
>
> They currently handle all this in two ways. One is memory. Some of them say, "Yeah, I remember." Other nurses take notes. It can be a little bit on their notes app on their iPhone, or sometimes they just jot down notes on their clipboard and put them in their pockets. But they make notes all the time. They make notes, and then they update the notes. They cross them out and make more notes. In a few cases, we heard about a product called Rover. It's an iPhone app that connects to the hospital's documentation system.

The diversity of these solutions—and how the nurses used them differently—gave Omer an idea of what the nurses wanted in a solution. But his biggest breakthrough came when he interviewed one nurse who had created her own solution.

> One nurse I talked with—she started by taking notes on her hand. She would write everything on her hand with a pen, then she would wash her hands, and the notes would go away. So, then she started writing notes on a pad. But as she wrote down more notes, it became hard to keep track of them all.
>
> Then, she came up with her own solution. She created worksheets that used a grid system to track all the beds and patients. She would use that to write what she needs to do. Even more interesting was that the other nurses saw this and liked it. So, she started creating photocopies and giving them to other nurses. That was her evolution of a solution for her Job to be Done. That was great to hear.

Learning about other solutions gave him valuable information about what these nurses did and didn't like in one. First, he learned about critical pain points that made a nurse realize that the way he or she was doing things wasn't working. Next, he learned about what would attract nurses to one solution versus another. Finally, he learned how nurses innovated on their own.

It was time to create a solution. Omer first broke down the key moments that would prompt nurses to reach for a solution for their JTBD. He wrote short stories to encapsulate such struggling moments. For example:

> When I get my handoff, and I need to remember what I need to do, I want to assign beds and interventions quickly, so I can get back to work and not get bogged down.

> When I'm done with an emergency and I've forgotten what I was last doing, I want to catch up with my scheduled interventions, so I can pick up on what I missed and not worry about skipping any patients.

> When I finish an intervention, I want to mark it as done quickly so I can make sure I don't double-administer treatments.

Omer described how he got these Job stories and how they helped him innovate: "These struggling moments came after I interviewed nurses and when I started working on a prototype. I wanted those situations documented so that I could make sure I was focusing on the right thing."

Where's the project now? At the time of this writing, Omer's team is still in production. They've developed prototypes and are now testing, shooting for a 2016 release date.

WHAT'S THE JTBD?

Omer described some great data about a JTBD these nurses faced. The struggles for progress these nurses faced seemed to be the following:

> More about: avoiding adverse events, not being the nurse everyone talks about, losing my nursing license, protecting myself from liability, being unfairly blamed, feeling like I'm helping people, pride in my work as a nurse.

Less about: protecting the hospital, protecting other nurses.

Based on what Omer told us, I would describe the progress, the JTBD, these nurses expressed as follows:

Arm me with what I need to manage my interventions, so I can focus on helping my patients.

There are a few reasons why I like this:

This JTBD can be solved with a change in hospital procedures and processes. Nurses don't have to be buying their own solutions for it. This demonstrates the idea that competition for a JTBD can come from anywhere.

It shows how these "needs" are not intrinsic to these nurses. Rather, they are a product of the health-care system these nurses interact with. These nurses wouldn't face this struggle if management had designed better processes in the first place.

I get a good sense of what life is like when these nurses' Job is Done.

PUT IT TO WORK

Begin by identifying a struggle. Start wide and get progressively narrow. The first thing Omer did in creating a new product from scratch was to identify a struggling moment. He started by casting a wide net as he sent surveys to doctors, nurses, and hospital administrators. As he learned more, he focused more. Eventually, he ended up doing one-on-one interviews with nurses who worked within a particular department (medical/surgical). These were the people who were struggling the most. These were his potential customers.

Understanding the struggling moment is a crucial part of JTBD. In a previous chapter, we saw how the creators of the chotuKool didn't focus on a struggling moment. They also jumped to a solution—perhaps because they believed they understood their struggling customers. Don't do what they did. Instead, emulate Omer: start with an open mind and resolve to stop discovery only after you uncover a customer's struggling moment.

Find innovation opportunities when customers exhibit compensatory behaviors. Omer discovered a nurse who shifted between various solutions for her JTBD. She moved from writing on her hand to writing notes on a pad, and then she created her own worksheet system. It was so helpful that other nurses had asked her to make copies of it, so they could use it as well.

Innovation opportunities exist when customers exhibit compensatory behaviors. The edge cases in which customers use your product might also represent innovation opportunities.

Always keep an eye out for customers who use a product in novel ways, combine products into solutions, or create their own solutions for a JTBD. They have all the trade-offs, necessities, struggles, and ways to progress in their minds. Why not take advantage when they choose to express them?

10 CASE STUDY: JUSTIN AND PRODUCT PEOPLE CLUB

What's the JTBD?
Put it to work

Justin Jackson is an entrepreneur from Canada. At one time, his Twitter bio simply read: "Professional burrito maker." In that case, his ten thousand–plus Twitter followers may have made him the most popular burrito maker ever. Never mind his prowess with a burrito tortilla for now. We want to learn more about his experience as a nonstop innovator. The numerous products he has made over the years include the following:

> Text Me, Slacker. An app that helps users engage existing customers and acquire new ones through SMS messages.
>
> Marketing for Developers. A guidebook for marketing software, apps, and digital products.
>
> Jolt. A guide that helps users come up with new marketing tactics.
>
> ProductPress. A plug-in that turns a regular WordPress site into a membership site.
>
> Product People Club. An online community where innovators and entrepreneurs can share their progress, give one another feedback, and track revenue goals.

In fact, Justin enjoys innovation so much that he tirelessly encourages others to innovate as well. At the end of 2015, he created the Maker Challenge—a call for others to join him in creating a hundred new products.

I first heard about Justin when I saw his short video about the Jobs for which he hires coffee—you'll read about that shortly. I contacted Justin to chat about his take on Customer Jobs. How was he using it? Was it helpful to him? Justin told me how he had applied Customer Jobs thinking toward Product People Club and also his book, Marketing for Developers.

In this case study, you'll learn how Justin uncovered a struggling moment that his prospective customers faced, as well as how he created a solution for it to help them make their lives better. You'll learn how he grew his business—not only by adding more features to an existing product but also by creating new products that extend the progress his customers want.

Justin learned about Customer Jobs from Ryan Singer and Jason Fried, product designer and cofounder, respectively, of the software company Basecamp. He said, "I saw that they were doing a Customer Jobs seminar at their office. I remember thinking, Oh, that's weird. They haven't done seminars like that before. That was the first time I heard about Jobs [JTBD]." Although Justin didn't actually attend the seminar, it did put Customer Jobs on his radar. He said,

> After that, I began noticing Ryan and Jason tweeting about Customer Jobs. Then, during an interview with Ryan, I heard him say something like, "At 37signals [the former name of Basecamp], we've been thinking more about why people hire our product—or what people are hiring our product to do." I remember at the time thinking, Man, I've never thought about it like that before.

> Their product, Basecamp, is a great example of Customer Jobs thinking. It's a project management tool. In place of that, you could hire an assistant to manage all your projects for you. Both could do the same Job.

Customer Jobs differentiates emotional from functional. Justin once thought of Customer Jobs as an exploration of functionality—as a lot of people do: "At first, I was just thinking about Jobs as, literally, utilitarian jobs. For example, I've hired people to trim my trees. I've hired people to fix my plumbing. I'm hiring this product to manage my schedule. I'm hiring this product to make sure that I don't miss any more meetings."

The more he continued digging into Customer Jobs, however, the better he understood the emotional aspect of Jobs. Jobs as an emotional desire for self-betterment are something that stuck out to him. This interested him so much that he created that coffee video. "I love that emotional aspect [of JTBD]. When people go to a coffee shop, they aren't just buying caffeinated liquid. They're going for all these other reasons." Some of his own motivations for going to coffee shops include getting out of the office to clear his head, feeling cool and creative hanging out there, experiencing the ritual of drinking coffee made the way he likes it, and feeling as if he's part of a community.

This focus on emotional motivation and struggle helps Justin create successful products. In particular, it helped him create Product People Club.

How do you find a struggling moment when you don't even have an idea for a product? The inspiration for Justin to create what would become Product People Club came from a moment of frustration: "I was consulting as a product marketing manager at a software company. Things were moving slowly with the team I was working with. I came home one day and wanted a distraction. I [thought], You know what? I'm going to create a new product." But at that moment, he neither had a concept nor knew what struggle he wanted to solve. However, he did have a few ideas of where to start looking.

For years, he had been active in entrepreneur and innovation communities. He had a successful blog, newsletter, and podcast on the topic of entrepreneurship. His experience of interacting with his community told him that a lot of people were putting a lot of energy into solving a struggle about getting started as an entrepreneur. To begin, Justin simply started observing.

> I decided to take a closer look at the patterns I had been noticing within my audience. I've been blogging, sending newsletters, and podcasting for a while. People would frequently write to me with questions or asking for help and advice. I had all this qualitative information, so I began looking through it. Could I find any reoccurring struggling moments that people were experiencing?

Justin was looking for recurring behaviors that signaled that people were struggling and that they were looking for a better way. All the while, he asked himself questions: "What do people—unprompted—complain about on Twitter?"; "What questions do entrepreneurs and innovators keep asking me over and over again?"; "What topics are talked about during Meetups about entrepreneurship?" He said,

> There were two patterns I noticed. One is that people were lonely. People who are working on products and building apps are usually doing it in their spare time. They're doing it in their basement, by themselves.
>
> The other struggling moment I found was this frustration people had when they were just consuming lots of content. They were listening to all these great interviews on my podcast, listening to

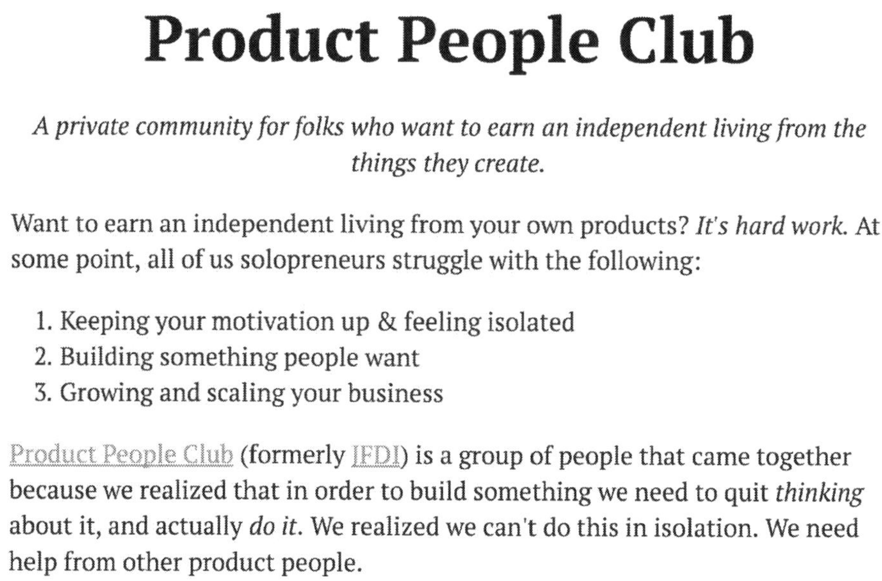

Product People Club

A private community for folks who want to earn an independent living from the things they create.

Want to earn an independent living from your own products? *It's hard work.* At some point, all of us solopreneurs struggle with the following:

1. Keeping your motivation up & feeling isolated
2. Building something people want
3. Growing and scaling your business

Product People Club (formerly JFDI) is a group of people that came together because we realized that in order to build something we need to quit *thinking* about it, and actually *do it*. We realized we can't do this in isolation. We need help from other product people.

Figure 17. A screenshot from productpeople.com.

> other people who are building and launching their own products, but they weren't doing anything themselves.

Justin was seeing patterns and getting questions seeking advice on two main struggles: (1) loneliness and (2) how to sustain the motivation to finish building a product.

The people he was observing were solo entrepreneurs who were passionate about creating something but hit these two barriers. Some were in small towns where they couldn't talk with anyone else about their struggles. Some exhibited concerns about being seen (or even seeing themselves) as poseurs. These barriers slowed—or stopped—their progress. A lot energy was pent up in these struggles, and something to release it was needed to get them unstuck. Justin said, "They just, they wanted to just fucking do it. They wanted to go out and build their own thing, but they were getting stuck. That's where I got the idea for Product People Club."

Justin had found a desire to change. Next, he wanted to test how many people were struggling and how intense this desire was.

How do you test if an innovation opportunity exists for a struggling moment? Justin believed he had tapped into an emotional struggle. Next, he wanted to come up with a way of measuring it. Was there an opportunity to create a product? As a test, he created a simple product: a chat room, capped at twelve people, that cost ten dollars a month to join. He put up a simple promotional web page that spoke to the frustrations and struggles of solo entrepreneurship and procrastination. The ad copy for the Product People Club stresses these struggling moments (figure 17).

Justin's simple web page had tapped into the two aspects of a JTBD: (1) the emotional motivation to better your life and (2) how life is better when you have a solution for your Job—that is, what it is like when the Job is Done. How did it work? He told me, "I posted the website to Hacker News, an online discussion group. Thirty minutes later, the product sold out. By the end of the week, I had a waiting list of almost four hundred people. It was clear: I had hit a nerve."

How do you dig deeper into a struggling moment? Justin had confirmed that an opportunity existed. Now it was time to figure out how to make Product People Club (PPC) more successful. He began interviewing his customers to learn more about their struggle: "I started asking my customers questions in a very deliberate way. I talked to people about why they joined." Justin asked customers questions such as the following:

How did you first hear about PPC?

When did you first think about getting involved with PPC?

Did you do any research before joining?

What was going on in your life when you signed up?

Justin was uncovering specific moments of struggle and getting a better idea of what exactly his customers' struggle was like.

> That last question— "What was going on in your life when you signed up?"—is gold. The last customer I interviewed, when I was asking him about what was going on in his life when he signed up, he told me, "Well, I had just quit my job. I had decided I was going to start building products and consulting full time." He then talked about being alone in his house all day, with no one to talk

to. His wife would leave for work, and he felt isolated, which is tough when you're working to start a business. He was also worried and scared about his future.

This is how Justin began to unpack the first part of a JTBD: the push—the struggling moment. The desire for progress for these entrepreneurs was "I want help managing the feelings of isolation as I start my business." Through his interviews, Justin could qualify what it meant to feel isolated. He learned that these entrepreneurs wanted to interact with other people who shared the same struggle. Talking with their spouses or neighbors wasn't helpful. In fact, talking with someone who couldn't relate to their struggle could make them feel more isolated.

As Justin unpacked their struggle with loneliness, he began to tap into the second part of their JTBD: how life was better when they had a solution for their Job.

> I learned that, when they joined the club, they would have this feeling of "Oh, finally! These are my people! These are people I can talk to about what it is like to have prelaunch stress!" Having the right people to talk with helped eased their anxiety and raised their confidence. It's that sense of community, friendship, relationship, and human connectedness.

Now Justin had two important parts of a JTBD: (1) a struggling moment—help me manage feelings of isolation as I start my business—and (2) how things will be better—I'll have the confidence to persist in being an entrepreneur.

His next step was to learn more about what these customers had already tried. This would give him more information about their struggle. His exploration of why they moved from one solution to another would also help him understand what customers did—and didn't—value in a solution.

Studying past customer solutions tells you about the JTBD. Justin continued gathering data about his customers through observation, interviews, surveys, and customer e-mails. This uncovered solutions his customers had already tried. Some examples of what he discovered as competition to Product People Club included the following:

MicroConf. A conference geared toward self-funded start-ups.

30×500. An online course that guides entrepreneurs from product research through launch.

Communities formed using an online chat application called Slack.

Creating a Meetup or attending one created by someone else.

One-on-one coaching from other entrepreneurs.

Clarity (which we featured in another case study).

Learning about what customers did and didn't like about the other solutions they had tried helped Justin understand what progress he needed to deliver. In particular, he started to pick up on another struggle taking place:

> [I also learned that] a lot of people in the community have revenue goals for their business. For example, they would say, "I want to do fifty thousand dollars in iOS sales this year." As I dug down into those things, I began seeing trends. One was a desire to have independent income. The other solutions they tried don't help with that goal. I felt that Product People Club could help some customers know how to replace, for example, a hundred thousand dollars in income.

Justin's exploration of other solutions customers had tried gave him ideas on how Product People Club could distinguish itself. This helped him know where to take his product next:

> What if we help you track that income you're trying to get to? Maybe you are closer than you think or maybe you're a lot farther and you should not quit your existing job. Right now, we're working on a feature that will help people track their goals. That's one thing I think about: how to help people measure their success as they strive to have completely independent income, only from creating and launching products.

Can more exploration of the customers' struggle to change reveal other innovation opportunities? Justin's awareness of his customers' struggle for progress led him to uncover related Jobs and therefore more innovation opportunities. For example, what new struggles do customers face once they overcome loneliness? What happens when they have the motivation and confidence to launch their start-up? Justin has some ideas:

> In terms of what's next for Product People Club, I keep thinking about how we can help more people build and launch successful products. A lot of people are looking for help promoting their product after they finally launch it. They have no idea how to get it out to people. That's an opportunity for another product that I'm exploring right now.

Justin is doing something interesting here; he's exploring struggles related to the one he started with. He started by developing a product that helps people overcome the isolation of solo entrepreneurship by giving them the support and confidence they need to build their own products. Once his customers have a solution for that problem—once they are able to get that Job Done—they need help launching and promoting their new businesses.

Creating a product for related Jobs. Justin knew that his existing Product People Club customers would eventually encounter the struggle of marketing their new products. Could he have something ready for them when the time came? He decided on a combination of instructional and interview videos, a book, worksheets, handbooks, and templates. This combination product is called Marketing for Developers.

Justin delivers his customers' progress. Justin is the most prolific innovator I know. Who else challenges others with, "I'm going to try to make a hundred things this year. Want to join me?"

Many factors contribute to his success. I believe that one of them is his ability to tap into people's JTBD. He can sense a customer's struggling moment, qualify it, and discover how he or she imagines life will be better once a solution is in hand.

I also admire Justin's skill in understanding the idea of delivering ongoing progress to customers. He looks ahead and anticipates the struggles his customers will face. He thought, After I help customers maintain their motivation to launch their businesses, what will they struggle with next? This is what it is like to think about delivering progress to customers.

What is even more impressive is that he understood how not to go about solving this downstream Customer Jobs. When he decided to offer a solution for customers to promote new businesses, he didn't fall into the trap of simply packing more features into Product People Club. Instead, he created an entirely new product. Why? He knew these solutions each solved a different JTBD. Had he done things the other way, he would have risked losing Product People Club's focus on the Job it should be used for.

WHAT'S THE JTBD?

Here are two quotes from Justin that I find most helpful when trying to understand customers' JTBD:

> Having the right people to talk with helped eased their anxiety and raised their confidence. It's that sense of community, friendship, relationship, and human connectedness.

> Oh, finally! These are my people! These are people I can talk to about what it is like to have prelaunch stress!

Justin describes some good JTBD data: he focuses on these solopreneurs' struggles, and he describes how things will be better when they have the right solution. And when I take quotes like these and match them with the rest of the data Justin gave us, I see the struggle for progress as follows:

> More about: loneliness and isolation of solopreneurship, sense of community and human connectedness, keeping your motivation up, not feeling like or being perceived as a poseur, "just do it," I'll have the confidence to persist in being an entrepreneur.

> Less about: attending a conference, taking a class on entrepreneurship, talking with a mentor.

With these data and the success of Justin's Product People Club, I'd phrase one JTBD as follows:

> Help me overcome the isolation and stress of solopreneurship, so I can have the motivation to finish my product.

PUT IT TO WORK

Justin's case study is a brilliant example of discovering an innovation opportunity through sniffing out a struggling moment. Let's see how it reinforces some other important JTBD lessons.

Innovation opportunities are found through looking for specific data. Justin realized he had a treasure trove of data only after he began to investigate innovation opportunities; however, he needed an effective way to filter it. He did this by asking himself questions: "What do people—unprompted—complain about?"; "What questions do entrepreneurs and innovators keep asking me over and over again?"; "What topics are talked about during Meetups about entrepreneurship?"

Investigate your data for variations due to special causes. For instance, why are customers using a product other than intended? Or if customers have never complained about it before now, what's going on? These are the types of questions that help you find innovation opportunities.

Know the difference between a struggling customer and a merely inconvenienced customer. Don't look for evidence of just a casual struggle; rather, look for people who were putting a lot of energy into finding a solution. In Justin's case, the community he was tapped into was reaching out to him and one another for help. These people were actively looking for a solution to a problem.

Perhaps the biggest challenge for an innovator is knowing how to determine if an innovation opportunity exists. It is critical to know the difference between a struggling customer and one who is merely inconvenienced. Aspiring entrepreneurs and innovators often move too quickly from observing a problem to hypothesizing a solution. Instead, be rigorous and look for true struggle. With the chotuKool, Godrej, Christensen, and Innosight jumped to a solution too quickly. Instead, they should have spent some time investigating if customers were really struggling and how intensely. But it turned out that there wasn't enough of a struggle for customers to buy a low-end refrigerator.

Great advertising comes from speaking to the customers' struggling moment. The promotional page that Justin created for Product People Club was simple. It didn't need lots of bells and whistles. All it had to do was to speak to the customers' struggle and show them how things would be better once they found a solution for it—that is, once they were able to get the Job Done.

Justin met these targets so well that he sold out his product in thirty minutes. By the end of the week, he had a waiting list of four hundred people.

Digging deep into customer motivation reveals innovation opportunities. Don't be satisfied with superficial facts about the customers' struggle. Dig deep until you understand the struggle, its context(s), and how customers hope life will be better when they have a solution for their JTBD. You'll see as you read on that a better understanding of the context of a struggle helps you understand how to grow your product.

Justin didn't stop when he believed he had solved a struggle. Even when he had Product People Club up and running, he wanted to learn more about the struggle. As we've seen, he did this by asking a number of specific questions, and that helped him develop new features and grow his business through offering additional products.

You can deliver progress to your customers' JTBD by offering a set of products that work together as a system. Perhaps the most powerful JTBD principle is that the study of the customers' JTBD is the study of a system. We'll look into that more later, but for now, notice two things that Justin did: (1) he created a product (Marketing for Developers) that customers would buy after using a different product (Product People Club), and (2) he designed Marketing for Developers as a collection of videos, reading material, worksheets, and audio material. Justin's combination of products works together to deliver customer progress. This is an important distinction of JTBD theory: it avoids the problem of unfocused "Swiss Army knife" products that try to solve too many Jobs.

11 Case Study: Ash and Lean Stack

What's the JTBD?
Put it to work

I met Ash Maurya at the 2013 Lean Startup Conference in San Francisco. As a presentation was about to start, I took a seat near the front of the room. Ash soon sat next to me, and we chatted a bit.

I learned a bit about his experience as an engineer and entrepreneur. In 2002, he had started WiredReach—a software product that simplified file sharing over the Internet. Eight years later, he sold it. He began blogging about his experiences starting and running a company, and he came across early writing from lean start-up pioneers. This philosophy suggests that innovations should be designed in small, low-risk steps that are tested along the way. It struck a chord with Ash because a lot of its ideas about innovation matched his own experiences. Inspired, he self-published his first book, Running Lean (later republished by O'Reilly Media).

Now he's building another company: Spark 59. It offers a collection of books and tools for entrepreneurs. In June 2014, on a podcast, I heard him share his thoughts on Customer Jobs and how he had been combining it with lean business principles. I wanted to know more about Ash's thoughts on Customer Jobs and if he had applied its principles to his most successful product, the Lean Canvas.

Ash used Customer Jobs to help him learn about why customers were churning from his product, about how he could deliver customers more value with new products and services, and about the benefits of interviewing customers who use his product in novel ways.

What is Ash's latest product for getting a Job Done? Most recently, Ash has focused on helping entrepreneurs get started on the right track and avoid what he calls the "innovator's bias." He said,

> It's when people get hit with an idea and then get carried away with it. They lock themselves up, and they start building the solution. They feel like they need to get it all out. They tend to be perfectionists. They spend a long time building a product,

exhausting all their resources—and then end up building something no one wants.

Ash is describing a scenario that happens all too often: innovators think they have a brilliant idea for a product, they spend time and money building it, but when they release it, no one buys it. At this point, they either give up or scramble to recover. Ash said, "Because [innovation is] such a long and hard process, many people also spend time trying to find the investors, or the stakeholders, that will give them the resources to continue building their product."

Ash helps innovators be more successful by helping them avoid the pitfalls associated with the innovator's bias. A popular tool he has developed for this Job is the Lean Canvas. It's a diagram you use instead of writing a long-winded business plan—most of which is speculative anyway. Instead, the Lean Canvas asks innovators to answer a set of important questions about how their businesses will deliver value to customers. They then go on to build the first version of their products.

Another problem that the Lean Canvas helps with is building consensus and a shared understanding around the business model for a product or company. But what about other struggles for progress? Has Ash found them all?

Can studying atypical customers reveal other innovation opportunities? Even though Ash had known about JTBD for a few years, he had never thought about applying any of its concepts to his own product, the Lean Canvas. This changed when he got an e-mail from Franco, a salmon fisher from Chile, who was having trouble using his site. Ash said, "We have the Lean Canvas as an online product. Every day, there are lots of people coming to the site and using it. When I read that e-mail from the salmon fisher, my first reaction was, 'How the heck did he find us?'"

Most of the customers who use the Lean Canvas come from the lean start-up community. Ash knew the product's audience had been broadening, but a salmon fisher from Chile was a dramatic outlier. This is the moment when Ash thought that a Customer Jobs approach could be helpful to him. Ash set up a call with Franco, asking him to describe what made navigating the Lean Canvas website difficult for him.

He was lost. At the time, the website assumed customers knew about the lean start-up community. He didn't know anything about that. Instead, he told me that he had been at a networking event a few nights before. He was talking about wanting to get a loan from the bank for his business. He thought he had to put together a business plan for the bank. The person he was talking with said, "Don't bother writing a whole business plan. Instead, go to leancanvas.com and create a one-page version of it."

Ash began to understand Franco's struggle: Franco wasn't sure how to convince the bank that his business would be profitable and that it was safe for the bank to invest in him. This proved to be a tremendous insight for Ash and his team— but not the way you might think. The value wasn't so much in that Ash had discovered a new Job; rather, it made him revisit a question that had lingered in the back of his mind: "Are we sure we know why people are coming to our website and trying out the Lean Canvas?"

You can gather JTBD data from customers who stop using your product. Ash and his team decided to do a new round of customer interviews to discover what Jobs customers were using the Lean Canvas for. They would talk with those who had recently signed up and those who had canceled their subscriptions.

They wanted to know the emotional motivations and expectations of the first group, and the second group's answers would help the team learn how, or if, the Lean Canvas was failing to make customers' lives better in the way they expected it to.

Ash crafted two e-mails. One was a thank-you to new subscribers, and it also conveyed that Ash's team wanted to hear more about what they hoped to achieve with the Lean Canvas. The message to those who had canceled offered an Amazon.com gift card in exchange for a conversation about why they had canceled. Though Ash got valuable information from both groups, the most useful was from those who had canceled:

> One unexpected thing that we learned was that customers weren't leaving because we were doing a bad job. They were actually leaving because they felt like they had been satisfied. They had created their initial business model. They had, in some cases, invalidated it and moved on. They didn't really see any other purpose to stick around and continue using the Lean Canvas.

It appeared that the Lean Canvas was, in a way, a victim of its own success. Innovators would sign up to use the Lean Canvas, get a lot of value from it, and then move on. But that wasn't how Ash had envisioned the product. The Lean Canvas had been designed for long-term use, but clearly, many customers saw it as a short-term product. What should Ash and his team do? Should they accept a moderate churn rate for customers?

You may discover that your product is being used for very different Jobs. If Ash and his team wanted to keep their customers, they needed a better picture of what Job(s) they were hiring the Lean Canvas for. More interviews brought insight.

One group of customers took the Lean Canvas as a starting point and then began integrating it into their own product-development processes, altering the Lean Canvas to connect to things like bug-tracking systems and company documentation. Ash found this particularly interesting. He had designed the Lean Canvas as a tool for entrepreneurs to develop business models for start-ups. Yet these particular customers were using the Lean Canvas to help them design features for an existing product.

Ash and his team were at a turning point. Which opportunity would they pursue? Should they address the high churn among the original audience (entrepreneurs)? Or should they extend the Lean Canvas to include customers who were using the Lean Canvas in novel ways?

Narrowing what Job(s) your product should be used for has benefits. After some discussion with this team, Ash decided to focus on their core audience: innovators who needed help creating and iterating on a business model.

> Our audience was already broadening on one end [more entrepreneurs were using the Lean Canvas], and if we went down that path of extending the Lean Canvas in all these ways [supporting corporations], we'd be catering to smaller segments. That is the point where you have to decide where your product starts and stops. For us, we said, "That's out of scope. If they want to do those kinds of things, there are many other options." We're not going to bloat our software with extra features. Instead, we decided to focus on what we do best.

Ash is doing something important here. Instead of trying to grow revenue by serving many different Jobs, he's choosing to focus on the few Jobs that he and his team can deliver the most value for. Instead of turning the Lean Canvas into a Swiss Army knife—a tool that does a lot of things OK but not any one thing great—he was going to evolve it into a scalpel—a specialized tool that is invaluable for a select group of people. The decision was made. Now it was time to figure out exactly how to grow the business.

How does thinking about delivering progress help you discover innovation opportunities? To figure out where to take his business next, Ash asked a simple but powerful question:

> To help us figure out what path to take, we asked ourselves, "What comes after that initial canvas?" Our answer was to develop two additional boards that would be used with the Lean Canvas. We wanted to extend the customer's story in a way that emphasized more than just capturing your idea for a start-up. It's really about creating a valid business model through experimentation and research.

Once again, Ash is doing something very smart here. His team had a question: "How can we increase revenue by getting customers to use the Lean Canvas longer (i.e., reduce churn)?" Many innovators in this position would be tempted to make changes to their existing product, usually by adding more features. But Ash didn't do that. The Lean Canvas was great the way it was. Changing it would waste time and money in overengineering a solution and risk upsetting the habits of existing customers.

Instead, he made his original product more valuable to customers—not by changing it but by developing new, complementary products. This is when he developed two more boards: an Experiment Report and a Validation Plan. In this new vision, entrepreneurs would first hypothesize and document their business models using the Lean Canvas. Next, they would formulate a strategy for validating their hypotheses, using Ash's Validation Plan to structure and document that. Then, they could run experiments that would either validate or invalidate parts of that business model; the results of these experiments would be documented on the Experiment Report. Finally, they would update the Lean Canvas and form new hypotheses as needed.

Ash both helped his customers be more successful and kept them using his products longer by extending his business with additional products. Customers stopped seeing the Lean Canvas as an end but rather as an ongoing companion.

Shift from selling one product to selling a combination of products that work together as a system. Now that Ash had added complementary products, he decided to rebrand his business. The Lean Canvas became the Lean Stack. This change represented the extended value that Ash's business now offered.

In the beginning, there was the Lean Canvas and the various Jobs that people hired it for, such as the following:

> Cofounders starting companies use the Lean Canvas's structured approach to help them overcome doubt and uncertainty.

> Entrepreneurs use it to avoid the mistake of wasting time and money building a product no one wants.

Some entrepreneurs, like Franco the salmon fisher, want help "selling" themselves and their businesses as investment opportunities.

The Lean Canvas is brilliant at these Jobs. The downside is that not a lot of people experience them, and there is a lot of competition among solutions for these Jobs. This means that the Lean Canvas, by itself, had limited growth potential. But Ash extended his business by serving up a collection of products that work together, as a system, to help customers make progress. This was how he was able to activate much more revenue potential. He said,

> Going back to the salmon fisher, yes, he will create a canvas, but what if he wants to raise money afterward? We could help him down a particular path. We might actually show him how to pitch the canvas to investors. There could be additional products that tie him together with people who can look at his pitch and maybe help him raise money. We're even developing features that help entrepreneurs run effective board and adviser meetings.

Ash's switch from the Lean Canvas to the Lean Stack puts him in a better position to help his customers with a larger JTBD: Help me become a better and more successful entrepreneur.

What is the future of Lean Stack? Ash continues to help entrepreneurs become successful. He is in the process of releasing his next book, Scaling Lean—a follow-up to Running Lean. He's also just released his BOOTSTART Manifesto—a rallying call for entrepreneurs, reminding them that there has never been a better time to start one's own business.

For the Lean Stack itself, Ash is looking at more Jobs that entrepreneurs struggle with:

> We've learned about many different struggles that people face: starting projects, big companies sustaining innovation, and even release management. As a result, we've discovered many different Jobs. We want to continue to learn more about those Jobs and decide which ones we'd like to help customers accomplish.

WHAT'S THE JTBD?

Ash's case study doesn't offer much data about one JTBD. Instead, it offers a lot of data about delivering progress for a higher-level struggle. You become better at seeing the big picture when understanding the high-level progress your customers are struggling to make. In Ash's case, his customers are struggling to become successful entrepreneurs. Along the way, however, they run into various challenges. A good example comes from the salmon fisher who wanted help persuading bankers that his business was worth investing in. Once he secured financing, he could get back to growing his business.

Ash's case study is also interesting because he understood that his Lean Canvas was great at helping people get their Jobs Done. So, instead of trying to make it better—which would most likely only make it worse—he focused on future products. He chose to offer progress with a collection of products that work together as a system:

Tools: Lean Canvas, Validation Plan, Experiment Report.

Books: Running Lean, Scaling Lean.

Training: Online courses, workshops, boot camps.

Each product is serving one or more Jobs to be Done. Collectively, they work together to help people become better entrepreneurs.

PUT IT TO WORK

Ash's Lean Canvas (now Lean Stack) is a great finale for our case studies on applying Customer Jobs theory. Let's review some specific lessons.

Grow your business, reduce churn, and capture more profits by delivering progress to customers. Nowhere is the Customer Job principle of favoring progress over outcomes and goals clearer than in this case study. Ash began his business by delivering well-defined, static outcomes: better business plans and/or consensus among founders. The Lean Canvas does these tasks beautifully—so well, in fact, that some customers don't need to use the Lean Canvas for long. In this way, the Lean Canvas was a victim of its own success.

Ash fixed his high-churn problem by changing his business from one that delivered a static outcome to one that delivers progress. Instead of solely focusing on helping customers create better business plans, he also began helping them become better entrepreneurs. This strategy creates more touch points between his business and his customers' lives, making it more relevant and valuable to them.

When you design a product for a specific outcome, customers leave when the outcome is realized. However, improving a customer's life never ends. As long as Ash helps customers become better entrepreneurs, he'll retain them.

Avoid overengineering your product; develop complementary products. If you sell a software product, offer different versions of it that tailor to different vectors of progress. Ash made a brilliant move that far too few innovators do: he made the Lean Canvas more valuable to customers not by changing the product but by adding complementary ones. Ash knew that the Lean Canvas was great the way it was, so changing it would neither make it more valuable to customers nor bring any new ones to his business. At best, nothing would improve; at worst, time and money would be lost in development, and the changes would upset existing customers.

As I keep pointing out (it's important), adding features to a product doesn't mean customers will realize more value from it. Remember when we discussed that a technology and innovation can be pushed only so far and deliver customers a finite amount of progress. This is because customers realize value only when they make progress with your product. Unless you can directly connect a change to your product with how it helps make customers' lives better, you're likely overengineering your product and wasting money.

Unlock your innovation creativity by asking, "What comes after?"
This is a question every innovator should ask about his or her innovations. After your customers use your product, then what? Do any new challenges arise when customers successfully incorporate your innovation into their lives? Learning these things from your customers will keep your innovation efforts relevant and profitable.

12 THE SYSTEM OF PROGRESS

Why study systems and the system of progress?
The interdependencies between customer demand and the producer
The system's four main parts
The forces of progress that power the system of progress
The system of progress is continuous
Is the system of progress new?
Put it to work

As I've noted, a customer's JTBD is part of a system. We call it the system of progress. Customers themselves, the products they buy, and the producers who create the products are all parts of this system. Understanding this is very important. It will help you find out what customers want, why they want changes, the relationship between customer motivation and the solutions they choose, and how demand is generated.

WHY STUDY SYSTEMS AND THE SYSTEM OF PROGRESS?

Systems thinking empowered the managers, designers, and engineers of Japan to create successful products that transformed the country from economic ruin to a global powerhouse. In the 1980s, equivalent teams at Ford Motor Company adopted systems thinking, thereby reviving the company, and created one of the most successful cars of all time: the Ford Taurus. Anyone who views innovation and customer motivation through the lens of systems thinking will gain a better understanding of how great products are created and sold.[51]

Interdependence defines a system. An important principle of systems is the idea that many, and perhaps all, parts have some degree of connectedness with each other. Something happening over "here" affects something way over "there." This connectedness is called *interdependence*.

An example of interdependence is what happened when farmers within the United States began spraying DDT—an insecticide—on their crops. Unknown at the time, DDT would get washed off crops and into rivers, fish would swallow it, birds ate the fish, the chemical caused these birds to lay eggs with weak shells, and weak shells prevented baby birds from hatching. The result was a decline in the populations of bald eagles, peregrine falcons, and brown pelicans.[52]

Studying interdependencies is an important part of innovation and JTBD. For example, Dan Martell recognized that Clarity was taking away profits from hotels, restaurants, and airlines. Anthony Francavilla realized that a theater production could increase profits by selectively offering discounts. Morgan Ranieri realized that he could reduce churn not by changing how his grocery-delivery service worked but by helping customers become better meal planners.

The system of progress is a way to understand the interdependencies between customers, their JTBD, and the producer. Once innovators understand the interdependencies that exist between the various parts of a system of progress, they can inform the producer—who may also be the innovator—how to create and sell solutions for today's demand and to predict future demand.

You do not help customers make progress by optimizing parts of the system of progress individually. You improve the system by optimizing how those parts work together. For example, a mediocre product that customers know about, can buy, and can use will beat out a perfect product that customers don't know about, can't buy, or can't use.

INTERDEPENDENCIES BETWEEN CUSTOMERS AND PRODUCERS

The two most important interdependencies within the system of progress are between customer demand and the producer.

The first thing to notice in this diagram (figure 18) is that the system is split into hemispheres. The two parts in the top hemisphere describe customer demand as a JTBD, whereas the two parts in the bottom describe the producer interacting with that demand.

The top parts of the system exist in the mind of the customer, who is the only person who can define their struggle to transform their existing life-situation into a preferred one. Yes, the producer can influence these two parts (as I'll discuss later in the chapter), but innovators cannot define the JTBD. Innovators may introduce new ways of living to customers, but it doesn't mean customers will accept them.

The bottom parts of the system describe the interdependencies between the customer and the producer. Yes, customers act when they search for, choose,

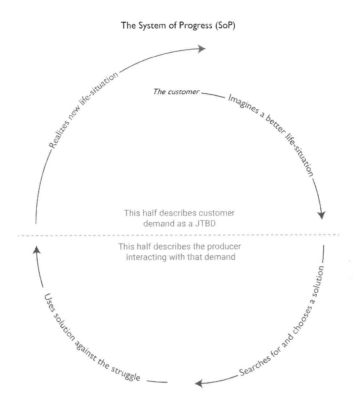

Figure 18. The System of Progress.

and use a product, but these actions are possible only when producers can create and meet demand, and helps customers evolve themselves.

THE SYSTEM'S FOUR MAIN PARTS

The customer imagines a better life-salutation (a new me). It all begins with the idea of a new me. Customers can be attracted to a new me because it offers them an opportunity to get away from something they don't like, or because it offers them an opportunity to grow in a new way. In terms of the forces of progress, these are respectively the push and pull forces. The JTBD arises when customers realize they don't have what it takes to make that new me happen on their own.

Your responsibility as an innovator, advertiser, or marketer is to understand this desire for change. How, when, and why did customers realize that they needed to change? If they are struggling, why today but weren't last month? Was there a change in what they valued? Was there a change in lifestyle? What was wrong with the solution they had been using up to that point?

The customer searches for and chooses a solution. After customers believe there is an opportunity to change, they need to search for and choose a solution for their JTBD. This is where producers—businesses that make and sell products—first make contact with prospective customers.

This part of the system is also where the richest data about customers' JTBD are found. Why? (1) Customers have their idea of a new me at the top of mind, (2) they are working hard to imagine how life will be better when they can find the correct solution, (3) they visualize themselves using various solutions, and (4) they calculate how or if a solution will carry them from how they are today to the better me they want.

For innovators, data at this part reveal what customers value in a solution and the priority of their values. For example, are parents willing to accept lower quality food if it makes shopping more convenient? For advertisers and marketers, these data help them know when, where, and how the producer should connect with customers. Then, advertisers and marketers are responsible for helping customers become aware of and choose the product.

Your goal regarding this part of the system should be to understand why customers are searching for and buying a solution now instead of a month ago. How did customers find and choose (hire) a solution for their desire to change? What were their hiring criteria? What trade-offs are they willing to make—that is, what are they willing to give up, and what are they not willing to give up? Did they try anything else besides the solution they ended up with? Why didn't those other solutions work?[53]

The customer uses a solution to start making progress. Customers have designed a new me in their mind and have chosen a solution. Now it is time to think about how customers use the solution.

This is the part where engineers and designers take over from advertisers and marketers and create product(s) for customers to use. They must apply their understanding of the customers' desire to change (the customer's Job), what customers value in a solution, and how customers expect to make their lives better once they incorporate that product into their lives. After a solution is

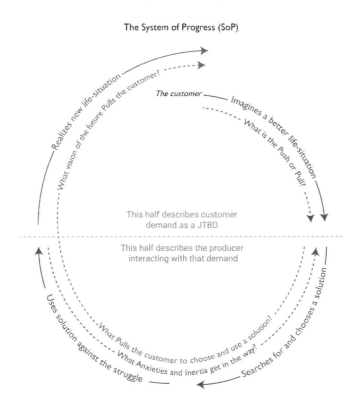

Figure 19. The forces of progress increase or decrease how quickly the customer moves through the system.

created, the producer should continue to monitor—and possibly improve—that solution by studying how customers use it.

Gather data at this stage. How do customers use the solution they've chosen (even if it's a solution created by another producer)? Are they using all of it or just parts of it? Are they using it in ways other than what it was designed for? Do they need to combine it with other solutions to get the effect they want?

The customer realizes a new me. Finally, customers realize that new me they've imagined all this time—or they don't. When they do, their Job is Done. If those better lives don't happen, they continue to struggle. They might be forced to combine your product with others to gain the desired effect, or they might put up with your product until something better comes along.

THE FORCES OF PROGRESS THAT POWER THE SYSTEM OF PROGRESS

Another interdependency part to the system of progress consists of the forces of progress that customers experience as they move through the systems they belong to. These forces are the engine that speed up—or slow down—customers as they move through the system of progress. They are represented by the dotted lines in our diagram (figure 19).

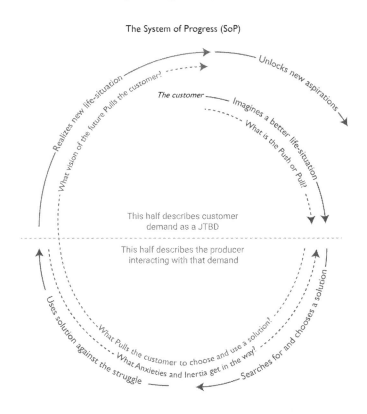

Figure 20. When customers make progress (get a job done), new aspirations are often revealed.

THE SYSTEM OF PROGRESS IS CONTINUOUS

There's one last part to mention: how the cycle starts again (figure 20). It deserves special attention.

Customers' ability to continue evolving depends on how successful they were at overcoming previous Jobs. Have you ever used a solution to improve your life, only to realize that you face new aspirations? The following are some examples:

> You buy your first car and enjoy your newfound independence. But now you want some help planning road trips, choosing car insurance, and finding a mechanic whom you can trust.

> You buy professional pans and enjoy your increased cooking control. But now you're curious about new techniques and recipes. You also need to figure out where to store those new pans and how to clean them properly.

> You've finally switched from a film camera and physical photo prints to a smartphone. Now you're curious about sharing your photos on social networks. And you're taking so many pictures that you need a better way to store and organize them.

As we can see, improvement in one part of life often has effects elsewhere. Often, when customers evolve themselves, even more aspirations arise.

The system of progress allows customers to evolve. When we add this idea of an evolving customer who continues to want and make progress, we end up with a helical structure like in figure 21 (imagine that the spiral builds up on itself).

The top part of the diagram illustrates how the forces of progress perpetually generate demand. The bottom part represents the interdependencies between producers and customers. Through these interdependencies, customers can make progress. The degree of success that customers make depends on how well the producer meets their demands.

The expanding radius of the spiral movement represents the customers making progress. This system demonstrates how one or more solutions can work together, or in sequence, to deliver ongoing progress to customers. The following is an example:

> A customer aspires to become a successful entrepreneur but struggles to get started. He turns to Product People Club to jump-start motivation.

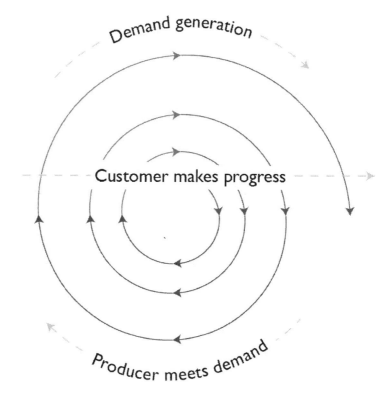

Figure 21. Demand is generated as customers make progress.

Product People Club is helpful, but the customer has some doubts about the validity of his business model. He turns to Clarity for some advice from someone whom he respects.

The advice obtained through Clarity gives a motivation boost and helps the entrepreneur realize that his business model is questionable. This is when he turns to the Lean Stack, using the Lean Canvas to retool the business model, increase his confidence in the business, and develop a shared vision with a new cofounder.

Next, it is time to release the new product. But how can the entrepreneur make sure it's a successful launch? This is when he turns to Justin Jackson's Marketing for Developers book.

Justin's book helps this entrepreneur become a better marketer. Now he wants help with improving the company's product with little waste. This is when he puts to use the Lean Stack's Validation Plan and Experiment Report.

And so on.

Our example shows how someone who strives to become a successful entrepreneur evolves because he or she exists within a system that perpetually propels customers forward.

New Jobs arise as customers make progress. They will use some combination of different products, so they can continue making progress.

The system of progress also illustrates why some customers experience demand differently from others. For example, some entrepreneurs may struggle with motivation but not with marketing newly created solutions. Conversely, an aspiring entrepreneur who fails to create a product because he or she cannot sustain motivation will never face the struggle of how to market it.

Another example of an evolving customer comes from BananaDesk founder Tim Zenderman. His product offers a complete front-desk solution (project management system + content management system + more) built for hostels. Over time, he has learned how the progress customers want changes as they move through the system. He told me, "At a high level, we found that hostels go through four stages of growth. The stages can take six months or five years. If some hostels don't make progress, they'll stay only at a certain level." Tim identified these stages as follows:

> Survive. This is the initial stage a recently launched hostel finds itself in. Owners need to drive enough guests to survive, and there are many ways (or hires) for resolving this Job. Some owners put posters up in the bus terminal, build a direct marketing strategy, or make alliances with hostels in other cities. Eventually, though, most owners find that posting simple photos and availabilities— by hand—on hostel booking websites, gets them the traction they are looking for and makes it the most effective hire for this JTBD (Survive).

> Control:Reservations. Once hostels start receiving reservations and managing the front desk more frequently, new problems arise.

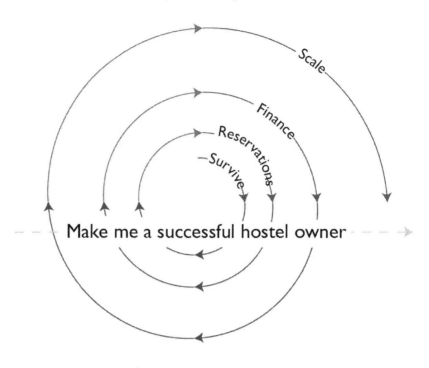

Figure 22. New challenges are revealed as a hostel owner makes progress.

In particular, overbooking becomes a problem. This is when owners need basic reservation management. This is also when BananaDesk first starts becoming relevant to them.

Control:Finance. Once reservation management is under control, they are able to handle a steady stream of customers. They're making good money. Owners now face new problems. How much cash is at the front desk? How much money did they make last month?

Scale. The business is humming along without much intervention. The owners have good reviews and a good occupancy. But how can they sell better? Revenue management, launching a franchise, or developing a direct marketing strategy (to lower customer acquisition costs) are all good potential hires for this new JTBD (Scale).

If we were to put these struggles into a system, it could look like figure 22. Tim also told me how the same product might be a bad fit for one stage of progress but then becomes relevant later when the customer does make progress. He told me:

> At the survive stage, hiring a direct marketing strategy is a bad fit because it takes a lot of time to correctly position a business. Moreover, the benefits from a direct marketing strategy take a long time. The hostel might be out of business before it realizes any gains.
>
> However, a direct marketing strategy is a great hire for the scale stage. The owners have the flexibility and time to invest in a longer-term strategy. This is also when improving margins starts to become relevant and is part of that new JTBD—something that wasn't important during the survive stage.
>
> The same is true for promoting their business on hostel booking websites. Such promotions are a good hire for survive, not necessarily for scale. If you look at just the functional need of these two stages, they seem similar: "I need to sell beds." But in both cases, the context around that "need" is quite different, and that is what determines the best hires for the Job.

IS THE SYSTEM OF PROGRESS NEW?

As novel as this cycle and helix concept may seem, it's not. In 1939, Walter A. Shewhart introduced the idea that the production of products should be seen as a system and that the aim is to improve that system continually. In 1951, W. Edwards Deming modified it and coined it the "Shewhart cycle" when he taught it to the Japanese. Over the next fifty years, Deming evolved the Shewhart cycle to describe the improvement of any system, from health services to management to innovation. The Plan-Do-Study-Act (PDSA) and Shewhart cycles were the genesis for improvement processes such as the Toyota production system, Lean Manufacturing, Six Sigma, and the Lean Startup (build-measure-learn).[54]

People mostly remember Deming's introduction of the PDSA cycle. What is often overlooked is Deming's introduction of the PDSA cycle as a helix. He wanted to emphasize that the ultimate intent is to improve the system continually with the intent of evolving it.

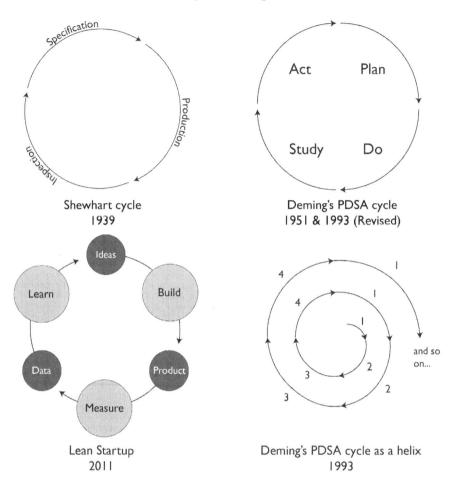

Figure 23. Different approaches to how a system evolves.

What is the difference between Shewhart's cycle and Deming's PDSA cycle and the system of progress? Shewhart and Deming studied a system that continually improves product quality through increasing knowledge of the process, materials, labor, and so on. We study a system that continually improves customers' lives through an increase in knowledge of their desires to evolve themselves, how they find solutions, how they use solutions, and how they make their lives better.

PUT IT TO WORK

Studying the system of progress—which includes customers' JTBD—helps you understand that your business needs to account for the interdependencies between the parts of the system. Here are some ways to think about applying the system of progress.

Grow your business by unlocking new aspirations and offering products for them. Justin Jackson's and Ash Maurya's case studies provide examples of innovators recognizing the new aspirations that their customers unlock when they make progress. Justin's Product People Club helps entrepreneurs overcome the struggle of maintaining their motivation long enough to ship their product. After that, they face a new challenge—promoting their newly released product. This is when Justin's book, Marketing for Developers, becomes relevant for them.

Ash's Lean Canvas helps entrepreneurs become more successful by giving them a way to create a business model that is flexible and adaptable. After that, they face a new challenge: how to iterate on, validate, and improve the business model. This is when Ash's Validation Plan and Experiment Report become relevant.

Get ahead of your customers. When they make progress, how will their interactions with the system of progress change? What new challenges will they face? Maybe you create a new product that meets the new demand. Maybe you add an extension that helps integrate your product with other innovators' products. Adding a hole at the end of your pan's handle does not help customers cook better, but it does help them hang your pan on a rack made by you or someone else. Either way, customers will realize more value in your product.

Think of your business as delivering a combination of products that work together to forward the system of progress. Your products are touch points between your business and customers. The iPhone is one of the most successful products of all time, but it didn't do it alone. Many people don't realize that the iPhone took off only after the App Store was introduced. The App Store and iPhone are separate products (units of output). But when they operate together, they help propel the customer through the system of progress.[55]

Moreover, as Apple's hardware sales slowdown—because sales for every product will eventually slow—Apple shifts to offering complementary products

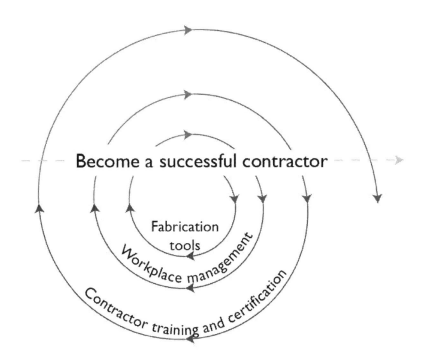

Figure 24. Demand is generated as someone makes progress as a contractor.

that build on the progress that the iPhone has unlocked. Apple CEO Tim Cook said in 2016, "In the last twelve months our services revenue [revenue from products other than the iPhone] is up almost $4 billion year-on-year to $23.1 billion, and we expect it to be the size of a Fortune 100 company next year."[56]

Another example is DeWalt—a company that makes tools such as laser specs, compressors, generators, myriad power tools, and contractor-training products. All these work together as a system to help DeWalt's contractor customers maintain successful careers.

Remember that the system of progress represents the interdependencies between the producer and customer demand. Innovation success comes from studying those interdependencies and understanding how they work together to help customers realize progress.

Identify parts of the system that your business hasn't considered or is overvaluing. Fill in missing gaps with data from the system of progress. Almost every off-the-shelf innovation or design process focuses on only one or a few parts of the system of progress. That isn't necessarily a problem, but it does create two risks: (1) innovators and producers are not aware that they are omitting necessary data, and (2) innovators and producers overvalue and overanalyze the data they do have access to.

For example, a company that has a customer- or user-centric process tries to fill knowledge gaps with ever-increasing data about customers. Therefore, over time, innovation efforts have created ever-larger reports that contain a great deal of irrelevant data about customers—reports that no one ends up reading.

Here's another example: a company that focuses on goals or desired outcomes tries to fill knowledge gaps by identifying an ever-increasing number of them. Yesterday, the innovator needed to identify a few goals or outcomes; today, the innovator believes it needs to identify dozens or even hundreds.

But you don't need to throw out your current design or innovation process just because it doesn't fit with the system of progress. Instead, learn to appreciate what data you are or are not missing and what you may be overvaluing. Adjust as needed. You might learn that the data you used to think were important aren't.

Find product opportunities by looking forward and backward on the system of progress. You can also deliver solutions for the system segments before or after any given segment. Most people focus on only one segment; we saw some examples of this in our first batch of case studies. Moving forward a segment is what Justin's and Ash's case studies show. They did that when they asked, "What comes next?" From my own experience, I'll give a simple and brief example of moving back a segment.

Before I created Aim—my advertising marketplace for real estate brokers and bankers—my cofounder and I had worked on another business. It would have been based on a product for mortgage bankers to process applications. Our initial investigation went very well, but during discovery, we learned of a bigger aspiration that mortgage bankers face: to find people who were looking for loans. Mortgage bankers first have to find those who need loans before they can process an application.

In fact, this desire is so great that some bankers spend hundreds of thousands of dollars trying to find people who are looking for loans. Our new information prompted us to change our business model and discontinue developing a solution for processing mortgages. As you know, we then focused on helping brokers remove the time and stress involved in finding leads so they can spend more time closing deals.

Here, my cofounder and I did the inverse of what Justin and Ash did. Instead of asking, "What comes after?" we asked, "What comes before?" It turned out that there was a much greater profit potential in solving for the latter struggle.

13 INNOVATION AND THE SYSTEM OF PROGRESS

The customer does not understand the system
Improving interdependencies within the system
When a system's interdependencies change
JTBD empowers us to innovate
Put it to work

> Any innovative company struggles with how much to listen to customers. Most realize that you cannot trust them to tell you what your next new product will be.
>
> How can people tell you what they want if they haven't seen it before? If we ask them what they want, we'll end up doing Swan Lake every year!

—Mario D'Amico, senior VP of marketing at Cirque du Soleil

An innovator's responsibility is to study and improve the system. Appreciating the system helps you find innovation opportunities and gives you the right mind-set to understand whether, when, where, and how to improve it.

This chapter will give you an understanding of what it is like to innovate for the system as a whole instead of innovating for only one part of it.

THE CUSTOMER DOES NOT UNDERSTAND THE SYSTEM

Spirit Airlines is the fastest-growing, most profitable airline in America. Its 2016 Q1 profit margin was a staggering 21.3 percent. Its net income grew 315 percent between 2011 and 2015. How did it achieve such explosive growth and profit? It combines rock-bottom prices with a terrible customer experience. Since it began, customers have ranked Spirit Airlines as the most-hated airline in the United States. If customers hate it so much, why do they keep buying it?[57]

Another airline, Ryanair, is similar. Customers also rank it as one of worst airlines in the world. It has even been ranked as the second-worst brand in the world. Nevertheless, its growth and profits are consistently staggering. In 2011, its net profit after taxes was €374.6 million; in 2015, it was €866.7 million.

Which voice of the customer should we listen to—what customers say, or what customers do? [58]

When Apple announced the iPhone in 2007, Microsoft CEO Steve Ballmer famously dismissed it. Here's how he described the "problem" with the iPhone: "Five hundred dollars! Fully subsidized! That is the most expensive phone in the world! And it doesn't appeal to business customers because it doesn't have a keyboard—which makes it not a very good e-mail machine." [59]

Many criticize Mr. Ballmer as being out of touch with what customers wanted, but they are wrong to do so. At that moment, Mr. Ballmer knew exactly what customers wanted; they valued low cost and a physical keyboard. Mr. Ballmer was doing what he thought innovators were supposed to do: empathize with customers, and then design solutions that serve their needs, wants, goals, and desired outcomes. And what was the result of Mr. Ballmer's empathy? Since making that comment, Microsoft's smartphone market share went from 12 percent to less than 1 percent in 2016.[60]

Then, consider Steve Jobs of Apple, a "monk without empathy." He changed the world with three massively successful innovations: the Macintosh, the iPod, and the iPhone. He also revived Apple from near bankruptcy to the most valuable company in the world. What was his opinion of customers? He said, "It isn't the consumer's job to know what they want." He also said, "A lot of times, people don't know what they want until you show it to them." [61]

Steve Jobs was notorious for being dismissive of customer input—and he was not the only one. Dr. Deming said, "The customer is the one who supports us." But he also said, "The customer invents nothing. The customer does not contribute to the design of the product. He takes what he gets. Customer expectations? Nonsense."[62]

Why would Steve Jobs, Dr. Deming, and Mario D'Amico—some of the most important innovators of our time—make these comments about innovation, customer input, and expectations? What did they understand that people like Steve Ballmer don't?

Customers know only what the system tells them. How does a doctor best serve a patient? When a patient tells a doctor she has a fever and stomachache, does the doctor automatically treat the fever and stomachache separately? Will he offer the patient an Advil for the headache and Pepto-Bismol for the stomachache? How about empathy? Will a doctor know how to help a patient once he imagines what it is like to have a fever and stomachache?

Or does the doctor best serve the patient by understanding that the fever and stomachache are not the patient's problem but only symptoms of the problem? The doctor studies the body, as a system, and recognizes that the patient's problem is an intestinal infection. An antibiotic should be administered to kill the bacteria, eliminating the infection. The body will heal, and then the fever and stomachache will go away.

Doctors treat patients successfully because they understand that the pains and discomforts that patients express are not the problems; they represent the patients' interactions with their own bodies. Similarly, the needs, wants, and desired outcomes that customers express do not represent their problem; they represent interactions between the customer and the system of progress. Therefore, customers' stated preferences are unreliable and why customers' "needs" and "wants" keep changing.

The customers of Spirit Airlines and Ryanair do not understand why management chooses to offer terrible customer service. They think, every other airline gives me free sodas. Why won't Spirit Airlines? Customers of 2007 expected a $99 smartphone with a keyboard. They were shocked by and did not understand the idea of a $500 keyboard-less smartphone. But fast-forward ten years, and that same customer accepts a $500 keyboard-less smartphone as "just the way things are."

If Spirit Airlines empathized with customers' needs, it might be tempted to increase legroom, add reclining seats, offer free drinks, fly to more convenient airports, or stop charging customers $10 to print their boarding passes. However, such changes would increase costs of production, and Spirit Airlines could no longer offer rock-bottom prices. Likewise, if Apple had listened to customers' insistence on a cheaper, low-end smartphone, it would have missed the opportunity to create a high-end smartphone that delivered progress in a way customers never imagined.

The needs, wants, and desired outcomes that customers express will change when the system changes. And there are countless ways a system can change. Keep in mind the dynamic of interdependence: a change over here can affect something way over there.

When you study customers' stated preferences—wants, needs, or desired outcomes—you are studying the interactions between customers and the system only at that moment. All those wants, needs, and desired outcomes will change when the systems that customers belong to change. Yesterday, customers wanted gaslight mantles that wouldn't set their houses on fire, cheap meat, and somewhere to get their film developed. Today, those same customers want environmentally friendly compact fluorescent lightbulbs, organic kale salads, and accumulating likes on Instagram. Why did those needs change? The systems that customers belong to had changed.[63]

These complex and ever-changing interdependencies within systems are why Steve Jobs said, "It isn't the consumer's job to know what they want." It's what Deming meant when he said, "All customer expectations are only what you and your competitor have led him to expect."[64]

Innovators must understand what the customer does and doesn't know. We must abandon the idea that customers have a laundry list of "needs." Instead, we should see customers as having only one need: to make progress within the systems they belong to. Any discomfort or frustrations they experience in making that progress should not be thought of as needs but rather descriptions of interactions between customers, their JTBD, and the product they've currently hired for their JTBD. For example, a car owner might claim that he "needs" more parking options in New York City. But is that really the problem? Or is the problem an expectation that it's a good idea to own and drive a car in a population-dense area like New York City? Perhaps the best way to help this person make progress isn't to solve the "needs" associated with owning a car; rather, it's to make car ownership obsolete. At the time of this writing, this is the progress that products such as Uber and Lyft are trying to make happen.

Customers can tell you of their struggles, how they expect life to be better, and how they interact with the products they use. But they cannot tell you what to do about it. This isn't because customers aren't smart enough. It's because they don't have access to the appropriate knowledge and theory. Customers do not understand marketing, design, sales, engineering, costs of production, systems thinking, psychology, and statistics all at once. They cannot anticipate all the ways in which their lives will change when they overcome one group of struggles and then face another. They do not understand the system of progress or why they can or cannot move through it.

Figure 25. Joanna increased revenue by helping customers find and choose a solution for a JTBD.

In other words, customers know only what the system tells them. This is something the customer does not understand, but you must.

IMPROVING INTERDEPENDENCIES WITHIN THE SYSTEM

It is the innovator's responsibility to study and understand the interdependencies within the system of progress. The system should be studied as a whole, and improvements to the parts should be done with the intent of making the whole better. Far too often, innovators believe that they can improve the system by studying one part—for example, the customer's stated preferences—and then making a corollary change to the product. Unfortunately, they often end up only increasing costs of production with no improvement of the system. The result is diminished profits.

I'll give you some brief examples of innovators who increased profits not by studying customers' stated preferences but by improving how the product interacted with the system it belonged to.

Joanna Wiebe: increase profits with new copywriting. Beachway Therapy Center offers a product that helps people overcome addiction. The center knows its customers' JTBD, and it has a great product for it. However, it was not happy with its sales. What could be done? Joanna made several copywriting changes. One was a new headline for the company website: "If you think you need rehab, you do." Another was changing the call-to-action button from "Sign up today" to "Does my insurance cover this?" The result was 26 percent more leads, each valued at $20,000 per month.[65]

Joanna improved the interaction between Beachway's clinic and the system of progress by creating a promotional copy that helped customers recognize that the clinic's product represented an appropriate solution for their JTBD. The new headline spoke directly to a lingering question that many people with addiction struggle with. The new call-to-action button was directly aimed at reducing customers' anxieties.

Me: helping new customers use a product. For a long time, FDT—a software program for engineers—had low adoption among some customers. I learned that these customers weren't accustomed to such a feature-rich, high-end product. What did we do? My team and I didn't change the core product. Instead, we created a video-training platform and integrated it at various touch points between customers and us. This was meant to help reduce the anxiety and inertia forces that blocked customers from switching to the product. Sales increased.

Even though no customers asked for this video platform, they instantly loved it. In this case, we improved our product's interaction with the system of progress by minimizing the demand-reducing forces—that is, anxiety and inertia—that some customers faced when first using the product. This was done without changing the core product at all; rather, we created additional products—a training platform—that would help customers move through the system of progress.

Bob Moesta: increase profits by designing for the system, not for customers' stated preferences. Bob led marketing and sales at a business that designed, built, and sold homes. The business wanted to offer a home that would appeal to empty nesters—parents who wanted to downsize their home after their children had grown and moved away. Two stated preferences from prospective customers were (1) a smaller dining room because they no longer had big family meals and (2) an expanded second bedroom so their children could visit. Bob's company delivered on what customers wanted. The result? Tepid sales.

Bob figured out the problem. These empty nesters were willing to change almost everything to accommodate living in a smaller home—except for getting rid of their existing, family-size dining room table. It had tremendous sentimental value because it reminded them of countless family meals. When it came to get rid of it so that they could move into one of Bob's homes, they couldn't do it. At a result, many ended up not moving at all.

To fix this, Bob did the opposite of what his customers claimed they wanted: he shrunk the second bedroom and expanded the dining room so that it could accommodate their existing family-size dining room table. Moreover, Bob added a big, old-looking dining room table to the demonstration home, for it would help customers visualize themselves living in this unit. The result? A 23 percent increase in sales.

These empty nesters thought that a small dining room and larger second bedroom would be best for them, but they were wrong. Why? They did not anticipate how hard it would be to give away their dining room table. How could they? Customers cannot see into the future. They cannot know all the ways in which their lives will change as they move through the system of progress.

Bob won because he understood that customers' stated preferences are unreliable, and that customers' needs will change as they move through the system of progress. Instead, he studied interactions within the system as customers moved through it, and he made a change with the intent of improving the system as a whole instead of focusing on just one part of it.

WHEN A SYSTEM'S INTERDEPENDENCIES CHANGE

All systems change. Some change slowly; others change quickly. How much and how fast the system changes depends on which interdependencies change and how many. A producer might be able to respond to changes within the system by making a small change of its own—for example, adding a new feature to its product. Sometimes, a big change requires the producer to respond with a bigger change, such as creating a brand-new product. Let's look at these responses in more detail.

Adapting an existing product to match a change in the system. For many years, customers used the FDT software I mentioned above to create games that were played on websites. Customers were happy with it because a healthy sync existed between our solution and our customers' JTBD. The system of progress operated smoothly.

The System of Progress (SoP)

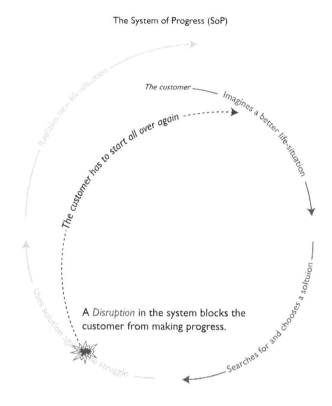

Figure 26. A disruption in the system of progress can force the customer to start all over again.

Then, smartphones came along. This affected the system of progress that our customers and our product belonged to. Now customers wanted help with publishing their games on smartphones, but our product couldn't help them do that. This frustrated them—and us! Our product could not deliver the progress that they now desired. If we didn't act quickly, a competitor would take advantage of this opportunity and steal our customers.

Fortunately, my team was able to adjust our product to meet this change in the system and fit our customers' JTBD. The system once again operated smoothly.

When customers can't get their preferred solution for a JTBD. You'll remember that a cofounder and I created Aim in 2013. But our product was relevant to our customers only because of what had happened three years earlier.

For many years, real estate agents and mortgage bankers had worked closely together to sell houses. The real estate broker would find people who wanted mortgages and send them to a mortgage banker whom the broker knew personally. This was how mortgage bankers used to get their leads.

But in 2010, US federal law made the traditional relationship between real estate brokers and mortgage bankers illegal. Just like that, the solution that mortgage bankers preferred for their JTBD was gone. That's why my cofounder and I created our Aim online advertising platform, which was like Google's AdSense. It allowed real estate brokers to pass leads to mortgage bankers legally. At first, our prospective customers were apprehensive about using our product because it was very different from what they were used to. However, when they were confronted with either engaging in potentially illegal relationships or using previous solutions they didn't like, we began to win customers over.

In this example, a disruption arose in the system of progress, and it prevented customers from making progress. They were sent back to the beginning, had to reevaluate their struggle, and had to begin searching for and choosing a solution for their JTBD.

FRAGILE INTERDEPENDENCIES AND CASCADE EFFECTS

We've looked at examples of innovators generating profits not by changing the product based on customers' stated preferences but by improving the system that the product belonged to. We've also seen examples of responding to changes within the system. Now let's look at two characteristics of systems that make products vulnerable to creative destruction: (1) fragile interdependencies and (2) cascade effects. Understanding these will help you plan and adapt for changes in the system.

Space travel makes for fragile interdependencies and cascade effects. The plot for the movie *Gravity* kicks off when a missile destroys a satellite. The debris from that satellite then destroys other satellites, whose debris goes on to destroy still more satellites. This cascade effect continues, eventually destroying the transportation that the main character had relied on to get home. If the main character is unable to adapt to all the changes, she will die.

In this example, the main character has fragile interdependency with the system she is a part of. In addition, a cascade effect dramatically changes her relationship with the system. In fact, the system changes so much, and her vulnerability is so high, that her chances of survival are almost zero.

What happens in Gravity can happen to products. A product's exposure to creative destruction goes up when it has fragile interdependencies with the system it is a part of or when innovators are unable or unwilling to respond to cascade effects within the system.

Some fragile interdependencies expose system parts to creative destruction. Every system is unique. Moreover, each system has countless, unique interdependencies. Some interdependencies are robust; some are fragile. For example, if you were to remove a strand of hair from my head, the rest of my body is barely affected. But if you were to remove my arm, heart, or brain, the rest of my body would be severely affected.

This idea of interdependencies and fragility also applies to the system of progress. In 2012, I left my job as FDT's product manager and once again became an entrepreneur; however, my departure wasn't hasty. Several months earlier, I had recommended to the CEO that the team be downsized and shifted to other products, that FDT be sold as a subscription instead of through major releases, and that advertising costs be eliminated or reduced. When I got the cost of production down as much as I could, I made one more cost-cutting decision: I fired myself.

Why did I do that? I understood that no matter what my team did, future demand for our product would diminish, causing a decline in revenue. And my job was to make sure that the product continued to deliver profits despite the decline in revenue. For that to work, costs had to be reduced.

How did I know that revenue would decline? I understood that the product had a fragile interdependency that would drag down future demand: it had a tight coupling with a technology called Adobe Flash. Any changes to Adobe Flash also affected our product. When demand for Flash engineers went up, more of our product sold. When demand for Flash engineers went down, we sold less. Therefore, when I saw that the demand for Flash engineers was on an irreversible decline and would eventually extinguish, I knew demand for the product would disappear as well. In other words, a fragile interdependency made our product more vulnerable to creative destruction.

Another example of a fragile interdependency is when smartphone makers use the Android operating system. At first, smartphone makers jumped at the idea that they wouldn't have to create their own operating system; they could just use Android. However, when they did this, they bound their smartphone's success to Android. This can cause big problems. Just recently (August 9, 2016), a critical flaw was found in the Android operating system, affecting nine-hundred million phones! This means that these smartphone makers and all their customers have to wait until someone, somewhere, fixes the problem.[66]

Cascade effects can affect the system. A cascade effect within a system is when one change in a system causes another change, triggering still others, and so on. A cascade effect contributes to the main character of Gravity being stranded in space. It's also important to note that the magnitude (and speed) of these effects is often nonlinear. They start out small, but over time, they gain momentum.

How Kodak succumbed to creative destruction is an example of how a business was at first unwilling—and then unable—to respond to a cascade effect. Kodak's decline wasn't just because of the shift from film to digital cameras; it was also because of all the downstream effects in the system of progress: (1) digital cameras began replacing film cameras for people's JTBD; (2) customers switched from stand-alone digital cameras to the cameras in smartphones; (3) digital cameras began to affect other solutions for other jobs—for instance, people switched from using physical prints and snail mail to using digital images, e-mail, text messaging, and online social networks; and (4) a decline in the cost of mobile data, matched with changes in online social networks, encouraged many people to switch from sharing images to sharing video.

Another example of a significant cascade effect is smartphones. Smartphones didn't affect only those systems that included phones as a solution; they also affected systems that included gaming devices, navigation devices, fitness trackers, calculators, flashlights, scanners, bar-code scanners, video cameras, alarm clocks, and so on.

The introduction of smartphones created a cascade effect that affected how customers made progress across many different systems. At the time of this writing, smartphones are having a tremendous effect across multiple systems of progress in India. Because so many Indians live on only a few dollars a day, they are forced to make trade-offs on the things they buy. Lakshmi Kumari, who earns $100 a month washing kitchenware in rich homes, says, "[I've stopped buying hair-conditioner sachets.] It was an added expense. Shampoo works just fine. I can do without conditioner. But I can't do anything without my phone. I can't hear songs, I can't surf the net, and I can't chat with friends." Venkatesh

Kini, the president of Coca-Cola in India and southwest Asia, says, "We are competing for the consumer's wallet not just with beverages and other impulse categories, but also with data services on smartphones." [67]

Admittedly, cascade effects are not always that dramatic. We saw a small one happen with Clarity. When customers switched from attending a conference to Clarity, downstream products such as airlines, hotels, and restaurants lost customers as well. Yes, the effect on those products is barely noticeable; however, it demonstrates the complexity of systems. A change in a seemingly distant part of the system can affect the whole.

Big things have small beginnings. Thinking about the fragile interdependencies within a system helps me become a better innovator. It even helps me as a customer. Should I buy a new speaker system that I plug my smartphone into? What happens when the smartphone manufacturer changes its inputs? Will I have to get an adapter?

Cascade effects are impossible to predict. You can predict a first-order effect. For example, when cars appeared, you might have been able to predict that nearly everyone would use one. But could you also have predicted nth-order effects, such as urban sprawl, Walmart, and car collecting? Probably not. In fact, I would have bet you couldn't.

JTBD Empowers Us to Innovate

JTBD empowers us to innovate in a world filled with variation and complexity. It does this not by offering us strategies on what our innovation should or shouldn't do but through equipping us with language and principles of customer motivation so that we can become better at creating our own strategies for innovation success. The following are some example scenarios:

> Sometimes, success comes from continual improvement of existing high-margin products that serve the most-demanding customers, such as IBM and the mainframe over the past seventy years. Or maybe you go the other way and create a feature-minimal product that offers rock-bottom prices and a terrible user experience, akin to what Spirit Airlines does.

> Sometimes, an innovation simultaneously replaces products that cost considerably more and those that cost less. An accounting

firm saves a great deal of money when it buys a PC to do the work of five accountants. At the same time, a PC is considerably more expensive than a typewriter or an Atari game system.

Sometimes, all it takes is a few tweaks that help customers use a product, such as what I did with FDT. And sometimes the product is fine the way it is, and all that is needed is to help customers find and choose it, such as what Joanna Wiebe did.

Perhaps the best thing to do, though, is to develop new products that help customers evolve themselves in ways they might not be aware of yet—such as what Ash Maurya and Justin Jackson did.

It all comes down to four points: (1) all customers want to make progress within the systems they belong to; (2) customers, producers, innovators, and products are all parts of a system; (3) understanding the system comes from studying the interdependencies between the parts, not from studying the parts; and (4) each system is complex and one of a kind, so solutions that improve them must also be one of a kind.

Let's go forth and become great at creating and selling products that people will buy.

PUT IT TO WORK

Here are some points that may help you apply systems thinking to JTBD.

Persuade customers to reject their current products by changing their JTBD. A great salesperson understands that customer "wants" come from the system, not the customer. So, if you want to change "what customers want," all you have to do is convince them of a Job that is worth getting Done.

Imagine you make outdoor grills. You want to persuade customers to upgrade from small grills to larger, more expensive ones. How do you do that? Well, you won't have much success if you just pepper customers with messages about how great your larger grill is or try to convince them that an existing grill is inferior. Why? These customers are fine with the way things are. A healthy sync exists between their JTBD and the small grill they've hired for it. Customers are making the kind of progress they want.

However, you will have a shot at selling a larger grill if you can convince customers how rewarding it is to host a large party and grill food for everyone. If customers agree to that idea of progress, they realize that their current grills can't get them there.

In that moment, you've changed the customers' JTBD and changed the system of progress they interact with. If they want to restore sync to the system, then they need a new solution. That's when you pull the curtain back on the larger grill and casually point out that they can cook food for twenty people.

Bring focus to which system of progress you're solving for by splitting up products that deliver different types of progress. For many years, DeWalt made radial arm saws that woodworkers used to customize shapes. In 1960, Black+Decker (B&D), the tool company that invented the portable electric drill, acquired DeWalt. In the early 1990s, B&D decided that its DeWalt division would serve a different system of progress.

B&D would continue to focus on giving homeowners the power to do small-scale home maintenance and fabrication work without the need for professionals. B&D's products include items for lawn care, preselected power-tool kits, and DIY books. Conversely, DeWalt focuses on helping professional construction contractors have successful careers. Its line includes laser specs, compressors, generators, robust drills, and myriad other power tools and contractor-training products.

When done correctly, splitting up products—or sometimes companies—to address different systems of progress is a good answer to the question "Which jobs should our product or business focus on?" Remember that a product that tries to solve many Jobs at once ends up not being able to solve any one Job well. When this happens, your innovation exposure goes up, and your business becomes vulnerable to creative destruction.

14 How Might We Describe a Job to be Done?

Try it yourself
Describing a JTBD

The Job to be Done is the big picture. It encapsulates why customers buy your product(s). Here are two ways this big-picture approach helps me:

> It's portable throughout an organization. Everyone from marketing to design to engineering can use it. It helps them work together.

> It's a good balance between high and low levels. It's abstract enough to give room for creativity while also offering boundaries where a product starts and stops.

This section describes how I like to describe a specific Job to be Done. It's not the "right" way because I don't believe there is one "right" way. What's important are (1) does it help you and your team work together? (2) does it describe a "better me" for the customer; and (3) does it help you avoid describing a product or how someone uses it?

Try It Yourself

If you want to know how I like to phrase a JTBD, jump to the next section. However, I recommend you try to describe one yourself. In this section, I'll offer you some data I gathered from an investigation I did on why people were buying products from Honest. Honest is a company that sells products ranging from household cleaners to baby supplies. As you read through it, think about how you would describe these customers' JTBD. The hint I offer you is to think about a JTBD in two parts—where they are today and where they want to be.

Honest's products. Honest offers a wide range of all-natural household and childcare products, including soaps and detergents, moisturizers, sanitizer sprays, cleaners, diapers, baby wipes, baby food, and vitamin supplements, to name just a few. Collectively, they are marketed as giving a family what they need to create a safe, clean, nutritious, toxin-free environment for their children.

Besides the products, Honest also offers their products through a by-mail subscription. However, their version is different. The customer chooses subscriptions to specific product bundles ranging from "diapers and wipes" to an "essentials" bundle that includes cleaners and bathing products.

Understand the customer's current life-situation. Next, it's time to focus on the forces of progress that pushed and pulled customers toward buying these products. In this investigation, I found two groups of customers who were struggling the most: (1) parents who had recently had their first child and (2) parents who have children with various environmental sensitivities.

Both groups described this struggle: The search for child-safe products left them feeling overwhelmed, tired, and scared. They'd ask for advice from their own parents, friends, doctors, community support groups, and the Internet. To them, it seemed that the more they "learned," the more confused they would become. Their own parents would say one thing, the doctor would say another, and the Internet...well, the Internet says that everything is both fine and dangerous. Everyone had his or her own opinions. Disagreements and arguments between couples were aplenty. These groups of customers also described similar struggling moments. Here are a few:

> Are there any chemicals in this baby formula that will harm my child? Is my child getting all the necessary nutrients for healthy brain development?

> Does my floor cleaner have chemicals in it that will give my baby a rash? This cleaner looks like it's OK, but it doesn't specifically say it's safe for babies.

> I finally found a safe household cleaner, but what about soap, shampoo, and baby wipes?

> My baby touches everything and puts everything in his/her mouth. What germs and chemicals do I need to worry about?

> I see hives and redness on my child. Is the sunscreen not working, or is this an allergic reaction? My information sources all give different answers.

Discovering how life should be. As I talked with parents who were struggling, I also asked them how they imagined life being better once they did find the right solution. The data were consistent and generally fell into two categories.

> Some parents felt as if the joy of parenthood were being taken away or reduced. They imagined that if they found the right solution for their struggle, they would have the energy to enjoy being parents and experience the picture of parenthood they had had in their minds when they first decided to have children.

> Parents felt they would get along better with their spouses. Some couples argued over which products were safe and which issues mattered. Did they need special soaps and shampoos? Wasn't it good enough that their multipurpose household cleaner was labeled "organic"? Preventing disagreements like these would enable parents to enjoy parenting together instead of them working against each other.

What was fired? The last piece of the puzzle is to learn what customers stopped doing when they started using Honest products. The results were consistent. These parents were combining multiple solutions together:

> Competing brands ranged from Huggies to Earth's Best to Seventh Generation.

> If they could, they bought multiple products from one manufacturer.

> They were asking advice and input from family, friends, doctors, parent communities, and the Internet.

Based on these data, how would you describe this JTBD? Do you think there are more than one JTBD?

DESCRIBING A JTBD

Here is how I described one JTBD that I discovered:

> Free me from the stress I deal with when figuring out what products won't harm my children, so I can have more time to enjoy being a parent.

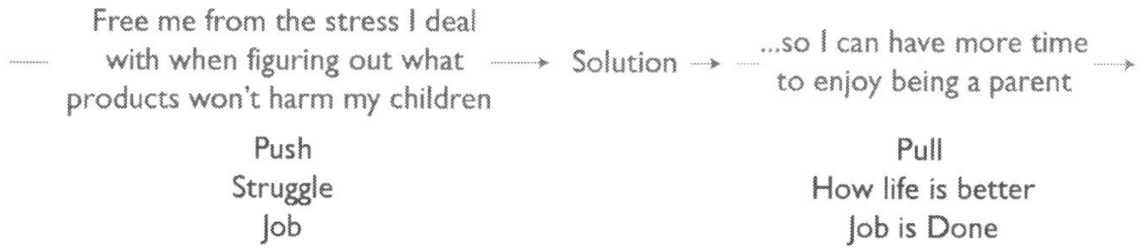

Free me from the stress I deal
with when figuring out what ----→ Solution ----→ ...so I can have more time
products won't harm my children   to enjoy being a parent

Push   Pull
Struggle   How life is better
Job   Job is Done

Figure 27. A possible description for a JTBD. Note the two parts: (1) the job, (2) when the job is done – i.e. when the "new me" is created.

When I put people's JTBD into words, I prefer to keep it simple. I create a statement that combines the forces that generate demand (push and pull) with the Job and when it's Done.

In this Honest example, you can see two parts: (1) free me from the stress I deal with when figuring out what products won't harm my children, and (2) so I can have more time to enjoy being a parent.

he emphasis on a struggle for progress is why this JTBD model often makes use of phrases such as give me, help me, make the, take away, free me, or equip me. These phrases remind us that success comes from the customers using the product to make progress. It also helps you think about how your product fits in between where they are now and where they want to be.

Variations of wording. I've used two other wordings. When you describe a JTBD, try a few different ways to say something, and use whichever you and your team prefer.

> Reverse it: "Help me have more time to enjoy being a parent, by taking away the stress I deal with when figuring out what products won't harm my children."

> Put it in third person: "Free parents from the stress they deal with when figuring out what products won't harm their children, so they can have more time to enjoy being parents."

Testing the JTBD. The most important test of wording a JTBD is whether it also describes the solution(s) it replaced. Remember our lessons on creative destruction and JTBD principles: when customers start using a solution for a

JTBD, they stop using something else. When applying this principle, we see that this description works.

When parents started buying multiple products from Honest, they stopped behaviors such as asking friends, family, doctors, and the Internet. The only time when they would go back to any of these previous solutions was when their expectations were violated. For example, one parent described how she bought a sunscreen from Honest without considering any other options. However, her daughter broke out in hives when the sunscreen was applied. This prompted the parent to go search the Internet and talk with people about what sunscreen(s) weren't safe. She also talked with her doctor to figure out if her daughter had an unknown allergy.

A JTBD to note. I chose to share this JTBD because it presents an interesting situation: I believe that many parents are hiring Honest—the brand—more than any individual product. When parents realized they needed a sunblock, they automatically bought one from Honest. This is important because it shows how fatigued parents were in their decision-making process. It also explains why the bundles are a great idea. With these bundles, Honest is telling parents that they don't need to think about what they need; Honest will take care of it. This delivery service also helps customers develop and maintain a habit of using Honest products.

I also like how Honest is offering a collection of products that work together—as a system—to deliver customers progress. These products act as touch points between Honest and various parenting aspirations. It's as though Honest is a software product that customers subscribe to, and each product is an individual feature.

Finally, this example shows a high-level JTBD. How high or low you choose to describe a JTBD is a design and business decision.

How you describe a JTBD is a competitive advantage. As mentioned before, I don't believe that there's any "right" way to phrase a JTBD. Such a claim would mean that there is no creativity in innovation—that we can just outsource our thinking to some model created by someone else. Every system is one of a kind, and every effort to improve a system should likewise be one of a kind.

15 GET STARTED TODAY

Influencing others
Learning Customer Jobs from others
jtbd.info
Customer Jobs Meetups
Contacting me

How you apply Customer Jobs depends on your situation. How much influence do you wield in your team or organization? Are you a designer who needs to persuade a product manager? Are you an entrepreneur or CEO who wields influence over employees? Are you a venture capitalist who wants to make better investments on behalf of your limited partners? How are your leadership and persuasion skills? Do you have access to customers? Do you have a product now, or are your creating a new one from scratch?

Each of these circumstances requires a different approach. Without knowing your JTBD—and why you hired this book—it would be wrong of me to tell you what to do next. What I can do is arm you with ideas on choices you can make. I can tell you how other people have solved something and what problems might arise for you as you engage in a course of action.

Regardless of what you do next, remember that everyone desires progress, even you. Understand that first, and then figure out the best way to make that progress happen.

Finally, this can be your last chapter if you intended to learn just the theory of Customer Jobs. If you want to apply Customer Jobs to discover innovation opportunities, please read on.

INFLUENCING OTHERS: CUSTOMER JOBS TOP DOWN

I've introduced Customer Jobs thinking to teammates as a founder and as a product manager. Dan Martell from Clarity introduced Customer Jobs thinking to his team. Morgan Ranieri's cofounder at YourGrocer insisted on applying Customer Jobs thinking before getting started. Here are some recommendations for you if you want to build Customer Jobs thinking into your endeavor.

Be a practitioner first. Then, tell everyone about the benefits and some practices. Dan from Clarity began by first being a practitioner himself. He introduced Customer Jobs to his employees only after he had successfully interviewed customers and understood their JTBD. When he was ready to involve everyone else, he explained the high-level concept to them, he gave them tools and techniques on how to interview customers, and then all of them interviewed customers together.

Are you being asked to start a company? Insist on Customer Jobs research. When Morgan invited Frankie Trindade to join YourGrocer as technical cofounder, Frankie insisted that they understand their customers' JTBD before moving ahead with anything. Frankie wanted to make sure an opportunity existed before he left his current job and would be spending his time building the right product since he would be engineering it. Not only did this approach bring the team members together, but it also helped them get started on the right foot.

Just do it. But separate the data from your synthesis of them. When I was product manager for FDT, I was responsible only to the CEO. He supported whatever I did as long as I got results. I didn't ask for permission to apply JTBD thinking; I just did it. I interviewed customers and gathered data, distilled their JTBD, discovered Job Stories, and presented my data and insights to the rest of the team.

The catch is that I made sure not to commingle my data with my synthesis of them. This gave the team the opportunity to debate my findings and offer their own interpretations of those data. I also never explicitly claimed that I was applying JTBD principles. I just used the language when presenting the data. Everyone felt involved, and they caught on. They applied Customer Jobs theory without knowing it.

INFLUENCING OTHERS: CUSTOMER JOBS BOTTOM UP

Other Customer Jobs practitioners have kindly shared their experiences in influencing coworkers about Customer Jobs thinking. Create a Customer Jobs theme Meetup, by David Wu:

> I first applied Customer Jobs theory and practices while leading product management at Meetup. Meetup is a product you can use to organize a local group or find one that you can join. I began

applying Customer Jobs principles in my own work and then introduced it to the rest of my team. Once we had made a few successes, we introduced our results in a presentation with the rest of the company.

I began by interviewing customers myself. Our company had a usability lab that brought in customers almost every day of the week for tests. It wasn't hard for me to talk with customers after they had completed a usability test.

I would talk with them about the first time they had used our product, the last time they used it, and what other products they had used in the past before using Meetup. Once I was comfortable running interviews, I began inviting members of my team to join me. They immediately began seeing the value in talking with customers about their desire for self-betterment and how they were expecting [their lives] to be better with Meetup. We were getting data about specific moments of struggle that would help us design new features and find the right messaging that would connect with customers.

My team and I had found value in applying Customer Jobs principles to our work. We wanted to introduce it to the rest of the company, but we had to do it in a way that wouldn't put people off. We decided to give a short presentation, at lunchtime, about what we had learned about our customers' struggles.

I created a catchy title for the presentation: "Why People Fire Meetup." The presentation focused on customers who had churned. I showed pictures of customers who had stopped using our product. Next to those pictures, I displayed quotes about the anxieties they had experienced while using our product. Most of the quotes were related to attending a Meetup for the first time or organizers not knowing how to plan a successful Meetup.

Showing the picture of [the customers] who had churned, along with a quote from them about their struggle, had a big impact. Right away, people in the audience started volunteering ideas on how we could fix these problems. There was a lot of positive energy in the room. When the time was right, I explained that I had gathered these data through applying some JTBD principles and practices. This got the JTBD ball rolling at our company.

Customer Jobs thinking starts with ideas you can test, by Dan Ritzenthaler:

> Great designers will want to understand their customer's struggle before they design a solution for it. Unfortunately, getting this directly from the customer can be hard. You're eager to go out and talk with customers about their struggles. Your teammates, on the other hand, might try to legitimize design decisions through their own intuition and anecdotal data. This puts you in a tough spot.

> People are averse to change. You're more likely to put people off—instead of winning their support—if you try to directly sell them on a new way of doing things. Instead, let them explore their prejudices, anecdotal guesses, and intuition. Then, reframe and massage their stories into a format that everyone can verify.

> Here is a way you can put your teammates' hypothesis into a format that you can all test: (1) How are customers currently struggling? (2) What is pushing customers to need a new solution? (3) Without describing the feature, how will the customer's life be better once the feature exists? (4) What is preventing customers from adopting a new solution?

> Now you have something that your team can verify. You'll be in a better position to ask your teammates, "Can I go check this out with a few customers?" Perhaps you can get some customers on to a quick phone call or send a survey.

> It's easier to sell "consumer research" as due diligence and verification of existing assumptions. It's hard to sell a new process framework. Plus, for people who haven't yet discovered the value of research, it's less likely to seem like wasted energy.

> Over time, your teammates will see the value in understanding the customer's desire to improve themselves. Then, you're in a stronger position to request JTBD-style interviews before flushing out a potential feature.

LEARNING CUSTOMER JOBS FROM OTHERS

You may want to learn more about JTBD theory from others and about how others have applied it. This is good, but it has challenges.

Customer Jobs has been around for a while, but it's currently fragmented. Customer Jobs began with Bob Moesta, John Palmer, and Richard Pedi. For many years, it was only a nascent theory with rough edges. These men evolved it as they applied it, and they taught parts of it to clients, friends, coworkers, and academics. The spread of Customer Jobs has been similar to the spread of information in the telephone game; every time it passed from one person to another, it changed a little bit.

This is a trade-off when a message is spread quickly, but the result is frustrating for newcomers who want to know which version is "right" or "the best." Even Pedi's, Moesta's, and Palmer's ideas on Customer Jobs have diverged. Today, you might think they are talking about completely different things.

I, myself, don't have an allegiance to any single "correct" version of Customer Jobs. I don't want Customer Jobs; I want the progress the theory can deliver me. My advice is not to worry about which way is the correct one to apply Customer Jobs thinking. Pick and choose whatever parts help you; however, I do stick very close to the principles and theory outlined in this book. They have been proven, through practice, to be reliable. I recommend you do the same.

JTBD.INFO

I maintain a collection of Customer Jobs-related articles at jtbd.info. I invite you to read them. I also encourage you, the reader, to submit articles for publication. How have you applied Customer Jobs? Have you created any tools that might help others? Do you have a story to tell? Do you have an idea on how to improve Customer Jobs theory? You can submit an article via jtbd.info by clicking the e-mail or Twitter icons on the front page.

My rules for publishing are straightforward. First, the content must be mostly original. It doesn't help anyone to rephrase what someone else has already said elsewhere. Second, contrary opinions are welcome and encouraged but need to be well formed and supported. Perhaps you disagree with the theory I suggest in this book. That's great! Just make sure your argument is solid and backed up.

Customer Jobs Meetups. A Customer Jobs Meetup (meetup.com) is a great place to discuss Customer Jobs principles and practices and to share stories. David Wu began the JTBD (abbreviated from Customer Jobs) Meetup in New York City, and now I cohost it with him.

Running a Meetup. A great way to run a Meetup is to introduce Customer Jobs briefly to anyone new. Then, introduce a product and invite everyone to think about what Job(s) it might be used for—that is, how it helps people improve themselves, and how it makes people's lives better.

A Customer Jobs Meetup will be most successful when you have at least four attendees. Or, before starting a Customer Jobs Meetup in your area, you may want to have informal get-togethers in your community. The following are some possible ideas.

Begin as an advocate within your company. Perhaps you can convince a few coworkers to meet after work or during lunch to talk about applying Customer Jobs principles to your business. When you become comfortable with this, invite people from other companies to join in. Exchange ideas and challenges.

Meet other entrepreneurs and innovators at other Meetups. Talk with them about Customer Jobs. If you can drum up interest, ask if they'd be interested in getting together for a Meetup specifically about Customer Jobs.

CONTACTING ME

I try to help anyone I can, however I can. As time permits, I enjoy doing calls and sharing e-mails with entrepreneurs and innovators. I encourage you to contact me via my website with your questions or comments or if you want help. If I can't help you, I'm sure I know someone who can.

I also enjoy learning how others apply Customer Jobs. If you have a story or insight to share, feel free to contact me. The best ways to contact me are through my website, alanklement.com; Twitter, @alanklement; or the jtbd.info site.

16 Appendix: Know the Two — Very — Different Interpretations of Jobs to be Done

Two Models: Jobs-As-Progress; Jobs-As-Activities
Do Goals vs. Be Goals
Jobs-As-Activities
Jobs-As-Progress
Two different, incompatible models
The Future? Use What's Helpful. Don't Assume Anything

Note: the content in this chapter originally appeared as a blog post on JTBD.info. It has been added to this second edition because many people find it helpful.

The popularity of Jobs to be Done has exploded in recent years. This has been both good and bad.

On the benefit side, powerful concepts like "progress" are disseminating throughout design and innovation communities. On the downside, because the phrase "Jobs to be Done" has evolved publicly and openly for quite some time, numerous problems have popped up:

> After Clayton Christensen loosely introduced the phrase in his book, The Innovator's Solution (2003), many people have offered different interpretations of Jobs to be Done.

> Newcomers are unaware of the different interpretations. This confuses them and/or discourages them from participating.

> Criticisms against one interpretation are mistakenly applied to both. This dissuades people from investigating it further.

The aim of this chapter will help you:

> Know the two main interpretations of Jobs to be Done.

> Be able to quickly find JTBD content that is relevant to you.

> Understand why people claim why one interpretation is nothing new.

Contribute and evolve Jobs theory in a positive, open-source way.

TWO MODELS: JOBS-AS-PROGRESS; JOBS-AS-ACTIVITIES

This chapter will focus on the two, main interpretation of Jobs to be Done. Each has evolved in different ways. And as you will learn, they are also incompatible with each other.

The two versions of Job to be Done are:

> Jobs-As-Progress: a theory that is promoted by Clayton Christensen, Bob Moesta, and myself.

> Jobs-As-Activities: an ideology and typology promoted by Anthony Ulwick and licensees of his patented Outcome Driven Innovation.

In an odd coincidence, these two different ideas can be represented side by side in an excerpt from Levitt's 1983 book, The Marketing Imagination:

> [The marketing imagination] resides in its implied suggestion as to what to do—in this case, find out what problems people are trying to solve. It is represented by Charles Revson's famous distinction regarding the business of Revlon, Inc.: "In the factories we make cosmetics. In the drugs stores we sell hope." It is characterized by Leo McGinneva's famous clarification about why people buy quarter-inch drill bits:" They don't want quarter-inch bits. They want quarter-inch holes."

While Levitt wasn't talking about JTBD, his two examples match the two different interpretations of Job to be Done. Each offers a different opinion on why people buy products.

Revson's customers-want-hope is about results from a change. I buy and use makeup for the first time because I want to change how others perceive me and how I perceive myself.

McGinneva's customers-want-quarter-inch-holes is about results from a use-case. I buy a particular drill bit because I want to make a particular hole.

Powers Motivational Hierarchy

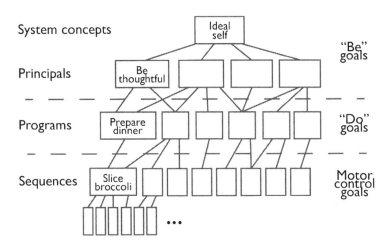

Figure 28. Powers' hierarchy of goals as represented in "on the self-regulation of behavior" (carver 2001). Also see "means-ends" analysis (Newell & Simon 1972).

Before we get into the details of these two interpretations, we need some background on the difference between "Be" goals and "Do" goals.

Do Goals Vs. Be Goals

Even if you forget everything else in this chapter, make sure you remember figure 28.

William Powers' hierarchy of goals (1973a, 1973b) is a widely accepted model of the relationship between the things we do, and why we do them. Not only does this help with understanding Jobs to be Done, it also helps in understanding other approaches to design and innovation.

With regards to JTBD, this model is a typology that describes a few important concepts:

The types of goals humans have.

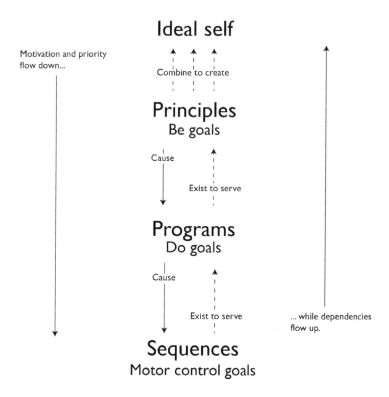

Figure 29. A dependency inversion exists within our goal system.

The priority order amongst the different types of goals.

How the goal types influence each other.

The dependency between goal types.

Here's how it works.

Different goals. Your ideal self is a synthesis of various Principles or "Be" goals. For example, you think of yourself as a particular type of parent or friend and having a particular set of personal freedoms. These Be goals are what motivate you to choose and carry out one or more Programs or "Do" goals. These Do goals are then fulfilled by Sequences or Motor control goals.

Be goals have the highest priority; Motor control goals have the lowest. Be goals are the core drivers of all our actions and decisions. This also means that, no matter how well a Do or Motor Control goal is fulfilled, it's a failure if the higher Be goal is not satisfied. It also means that a Do goal doesn't have to be successfully executed to fulfill a Be goal.

A fancy way of saying this, is to say that a dependency inversion exists in our goal systems (figure 29). High level goals don't need low level goals, but low-level goals need high level goals.

For example, suppose your goal is to be thoughtful for your family. To fulfill this goal, you choose the activity cook.

However, the fulfillment of be thoughtful isn't dependent on the success or failure of cook dinner.

It's possible that you brilliantly cook dinner, but if your family would have preferred going to a restaurant, you failed. On the other hand, you could be totally unsuccessful at the cook dinner activity, but if your family finds the gesture endearing and thinks of you as being thoughtful anyway, then the activity was a success.

Taken even further, Be goals can be fulfilled without even needing to engage in any activity (Carver 2001). For example, suppose you live in a neighborhood that has high crime. This high crime made you feel unsafe (an unattained Be goal). Then, without any action on your part, the local police start 24/7 patrolling. Immediately, you start feeling safer. Over time, crime reduces, and you become safe. Your life-situation (your collection of Be goals) has changed even though you didn't carry out any activities or tasks (Do or Motor control goals).

Be goals are the most stable; Do and Motor control goals are transitory. Be goals are states of self-perception. They are entirely emotional (or psychological if you prefer that word). Do and Motor control goals are purely functional and are technology dependent. They are things you do to fulfill a Be goal.

Stated another way: You don't ultimately want to achieve the Do and Motor goals; you want the Be goals.

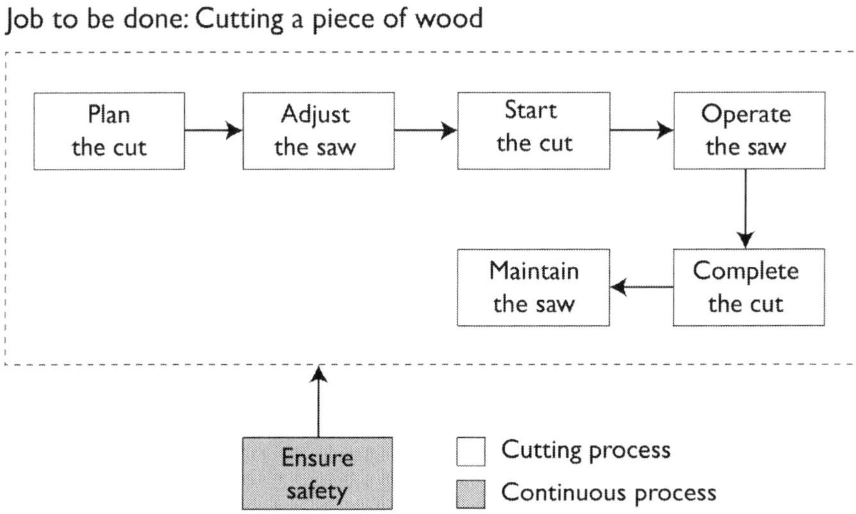

Job to be done: Cutting a piece of wood

Figure 30. Ulwick sees jobs as activities and tasks (Ulwick 2005).

This reason—along with the fact that our self-perception changes slowly—means that Be goals are more stable than Do and Motor control goals. As illustrated by Powers and Carver, humans switch between and even combine multiple Do and Motor control goals as they aim to fulfill Be goals. For example, in my pursuit to "be thoughtful", I might cook dinner, buy wine, write a poem, and make a home video. A real example of this behavior appears later in the article.

Now we're ready to get into the two interpretations of JTBD.

JOBS-AS-ACTIVITIES

Determining how Jobs came to be associated with tasks and activities is tricky. The phrase Jobs to be Done, with regards to an innovation ideology, was first used by Clayton Christensen (Christensen 2003). In it he references:

> Rick Pedi as having "coined for us the language Jobs to be Done" (this account is expanded in Christensen's 2016 book).

Anthony Ulwick of Strategyn as having "used a very similar concept in his consulting work, using the phrase outcomes that customers are seeking."

James J. Gibson's theory of affordances as "being a concept that mirrors what we term jobs or outcomes."

However, Christensen never defined what a Job to be Done was, nor used it with rigor. Christensen gives examples of Job such as make the commute more interesting, placate children, feel like loving parents, and use small snippets of time productively (Christensen 2003). If you were to put these examples against Powers' goal hierarchy, they range from low-level Motor control goals to high level Be goals.

I asked Clay's team about this discrepancy when I met with them to develop the Jobs-As-Progress model. Their answer was that, back in 2003 they were just starting to develop the theory. As a result, some ambiguity existed.

The most notable instance of interpreting Jobs-As-Activities is from Anthony Ulwick (Ulwick 2005, 2016).

What is it? Ulwick is the primary proponent of the idea of Jobs-As-Activities. As an example of this thinking, Ulwick cites McGinneva's "Customers want a quarter inch hole…" quote (Ulwick 2016).

In his 2005 book, Ulwick describes a Job to be Done as:

> [Companies] must know which jobs their customers are trying to get done (that is, the tasks or activities customers are trying to carry out).

In his 2016 book, he defines a Job to be Done as:

> A task, goal or objective a person is trying to accomplish or a problem they are trying to resolve. A job can be functional, emotional or associated with product consumption (consumption chain jobs).

A Job to be Done is then described in terms of a Job Map:

Analysis of hundreds of jobs has revealed that all jobs consist of some or all of the eight fundamental process steps: define, locate, prepare, confirm, execute, monitor, modify and conclude (see the universal job map).

Ulwick defines Jobs to be Done as:

Jobs-to-be-Done Theory provides a framework for (i) categorizing, defining, capturing, and organizing all your customer's needs, and (ii) tying customer-defined performance metrics (in the form of desired outcome statements) to the Job-to-be-Done.

With regards to being called a "theory", the description given is not of a theory, but of an Ideology and Typology. A theory is a hypothesis of how and why a natural or social phenomenon happens—e.g. evolution, gravity, bending of space-time. On the other hand, an ideology is a belief system (e.g. a strategy) and a typology is a categorization schema (Bacharach 1989, Bhattacherjee 2012, Colquitt 2007).

Ulwick's Jobs-As-Activities suggests that customers want to do these activities. Examples of Jobs in this model include listen to music, drill a quarter-inch hole, storing-retrieving music, and cutting a piece of wood. As a result, the activity becomes the fundamental unit of analysis. Any emotional considerations are secondary to this core, functional Job:

Emotional jobs define how customers want to feel or avoid feeling as a result of executing the core functional job. Social jobs define how the customer wants to be perceived by others.

The core functional job is the anchor around which all other needs are defined. It is defined first, then the emotional, related and consumption chain jobs are defined relative to the core functional job.

Within the Powers model, a Job to be Done in this interpretation is a Program made up of Sequences—or Do goals made up of Motor control goals.

What is it based upon or similar to? Those who have experience in Goal-Directed Design, Cognitive Task Analysis, Hierarchical Task Analysis, Human Computer Interaction (HCI), Use Cases, or Activity-Centered Design will

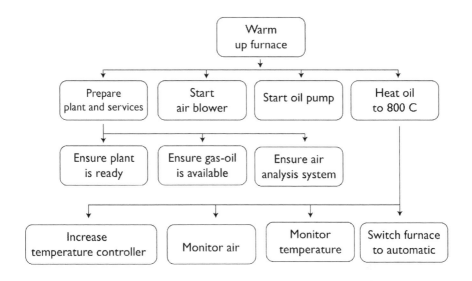

Figure 31. "Warm up furnace" is an example of task analysis. Ulwick's idea of jobs to be done is similar to task analysis.

recognize this interpretation of JTBD as similar to what they are already doing (figure 31), and the notion of "desired outcomes" is also similar to Sayan Chatterjee's paper, Delivering desired outcomes efficiently: the creative key to competitive strategy (Chatterjee 1998).

The many similarities of Jobs-As-Activities model has with these other existing ideas is why a lot of people claim that Jobs to be Done is nothing new.

For example, Ulwick's Job Map is very similar to Norman's Seven Stages of Action (figure 32). They're not exactly the same, but they are strikingly similar. Both are based upon the idea of a person physically interacting with a technology through three phases: planning, doing, and evaluating.

Both Don Norman and Anthony Ulwick even use listen to music as an example of an activity. Here's how Norman describes the activity of listen to music in his 2013 edition of his 1988 book:

> Focusing upon tasks is too limiting. Apple's success with its music player, the iPod, was because Apple supported the entire activity involved in listening to music: discovering it, purchasing it,

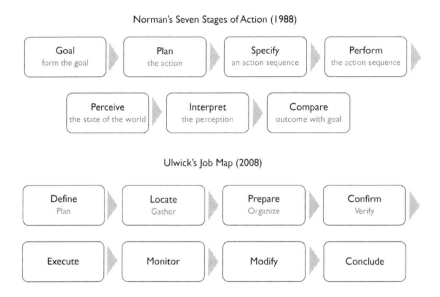

Figure 32. Don Norman's action model (top) is very similar to Ulwick's job map (bottom).

getting it into the music player, developing playlists (that could be shared), and listening to the music.

The biggest difference between Ulwick's Jobs-As-Activities model and HCI, Activity Centered Design, Goal-Directed Design, Cognitive Tasks analysis, and Use Cases is the addition of a business strategy layer. Ulwick's ideology suggests that businesses should focus on creating technologies that help consumers better execute tasks and activities (Ulwick 2016):

New products and services win in the marketplace if they help customers get a job done better (faster, more predictably, with higher output) and / or more cheaply.

Jobs-As-Progress

The first mention of Jobs as Progress is in the Jobs to be Done Handbook (Spiek & Moesta 2014). But this book was about an interview method and doesn't get into Customer Jobs theory. Currently, there are only two books that focus on Jobs as Progress and develop it as a theory: this book and Competing Against Luck (Christensen, Dillon, Duncan, Hall 2016).

Figure 33. A visualization of a Job to be Done and "progress".

In *Competing Against Luck* Christensen writes:

> It was Bob and his partner Rick Pedi who first brought me the puzzle that eventually led to the Theory of Jobs to Be Done and his work in the years since has helped shape it.

No references to Gibson, Ulwick, affordances, or desired outcomes appear in Christensen's *Competing Against Luck*. Instead, Christensen replaces the idea that customers want "outcomes" with customers want "progress". This Jobs-As-Progress model is the version Christensen, Moesta, and I promote.

What is it? Jobs-As-Progress is a theory only. Theory tells you how and why things happen, not what you should do about it. Theory is descriptive, not prescriptive. Jobs-As-Progress aims to answer several social phenomena such as:

> What causes someone to purchase a product for the first time?

> Why and how do consumers use markets to adapt in a changing world.

> Why and how do consumers shop (search for new products, services, and technologies)?

> Why and how do consumers switch between products?

The Jobs-As-Progress model suggests (hypothesizes) that a consumer will look for, buy, and use a product for the first time when a discrepancy exists between how things are today and how they want them to be in the future (recall Revlon's "in the drug store we sell hope..." quote and Powers' "Be" goal). Jobs-As-Progress is about a consumer's desire to use markets with the aim of resolving a Be goal discrepancy.

Figure 34. In "the why before the why", basecamp founder Jason Fried writes about four jobs (Be goal discrepancies) that cause people to seek out solution that would enable them to change their life-situation.

Two definitions of a Job to be Done in this model are:

> We define a "job" as the progress that a person is trying to make in a particular circumstance (Christensen 2016).

> A Job to be Done is the process a consumer goes through whenever she aims to transform her existing life-situation into a preferred one but cannot because constraints are stopping her (Klement 2016).

One key to this model is to recognize that Jobs-As-Progress is about understanding why consumers change their historical purchase patterns—i.e. why they would stop using product X and start using product Y. Understanding what conditions must exist for this behavior change is important. If you want people to start using your product (i.e. create growth), then you're gonna have

Figure 35. Dan Martell of clarity (clarity.fm) applied a jobs-as-progress model to grow and eventually sell his business. He understood that consumers were trying to resolve a be goal discrepancy, and that various solutions could be used to resolve it.

to persuade them to stop using the products they use today and start using your product.

The other key to this model is to recognize that it's about unattained Be goals (Figure 34). It's not about Do or Motor control goals. Jobs-As-

Progress recognizes that tasks and activities are a means to an end only. They do not represent what consumers want.

This realization helps us understand how consumers see and use markets. Until the Jobs-As-Progress model came along, most companies restricted competition to products that shared functionality (e.g. products that "cut a straight line"). However, because customers see tasks and activities as a means to end only, consumers end up considering products and services that vary greatly on functionality.

This is clear in the Clarity case study from this book. In this example, Clarity founder Dan Martell learned that a lot of his customers were coming to Clarity because they had a Be goal discrepancy around being motivated and inspired. This discrepancy caused them to investigate and evaluate activities that ranged from "attend to a conference" to "video chat with a famous person". Even though these solutions offer wildly different activities and are functionally different, they all competed in helping the consumer attain a particular set of Be goals (figure 34).

The Jobs-as-Progress model suggests that a great deal of innovation is about eliminating tasks and activities—not designing for them. IKEA's innovation was to create furniture that you could order and assemble yourself without needing to "cut a straight line", "drill a quarter inch hole", or even "want a quarter inch hole".

Moreover, in 2017, IKEA bought Task Rabbit. Why? Because they also understand that people don't want to "assemble/build furniture" either.

Rather, they want to be organized, express their individuality, and feel comfortable in their home.

What is it based upon or similar to? The theoretical basis of Jobs-As-Progress draws from many sources—too many to list here. The most import parts (humans as goal-directed organisms that self-regulate discrepancies via feedback loops) stems from people such as Norbert Wiener (1961), Herbert Simon (1996), Albert Bandura (1997), Charles S. Carver (2001), and William Powers (1972).

I am not aware of these ideas as having been used within the context of innovation or design. The closest thing to it would be Cooper's Goal-Directed Design and Hassenzahl's Experience Design (Hassenzahl 2010). However, even these are different. Goal-Directed Design is a method while Experience Design is an ideology. Neither of these aims to explain why or how any natural or social phenomena happen.

TWO DIFFERENT, INCOMPATIBLE MODELS

If it isn't clear, these are two different, and incompatible, interpretations of why we buy and use products.

The Jobs-As-Activities model suggests that customers want to engage in the activity; therefore, your efforts should be to improve that activity.

Whereas the Jobs-As-Progress model suggests that there's nothing functional or activity related about a JTBD. Why? Because it is technologies that function,

Consumers don't want this...

...they want this

Innovation should be about reducing or eliminating (not improving) this...

...so consmers can have more of this

Figure 36. The Jobs–as–Progress model suggests that we create technologies, so we can skip having to "do things" and have more time to enjoy a particular life-situation.

not our desires. Don Norman (1988) also offers his opinion about focusing on tasks or activities only:

> Most innovation is done as an incremental enhancement of existing products. What about radical ideas, ones that introduce new product categories to the marketplace? These come about by reconsidering the goals, and always asking why the real goal is: what is called root cause analysis.

> Harvard Business School marketing professor Theodore Levitt once pointed out, "People don't want to buy a quarter-inch drill. They want a quarter-inch hole!" Levitt's example of the drill implying that the goal is really a hole is only partially correct, however. When people go to a store to buy a drill, that is not their real goal. But why would anyone want a quarter-inch hole? Clearly that is an intermediate goal. Perhaps they wanted to hang shelves on the wall. Levitt stopped too soon.

> Once you realize that they don't really want the drill, you realize that perhaps they don't really want the hole, either: they want to install their bookshelves. Why not develop methods that don't require holes? Or perhaps books that don't require bookshelves. (Yes, I know: electronic books, e-books.)

Rather, a consumer's ultimate motivation is to regulate a discrepancy they have amongst Be goals. e.g. help me become financially stable, make me confident and impress others. In their pursuit of this goal, consumers may engage in one or more activities…or maybe they don't engage in any activity at all.

For example, the Jobs-As-Progress models suggest that people don't want to mow the lawn. They do so only because they own grass and grass grows (and dies). Avoiding having to "mow the lawn" is why innovations such as lawn-care services, automated lawn mowers, and field turf (fake grass) exist. Perhaps one day GMO grass will be created that won't ever have to be cut.

CHALLENGES IN UNDERSTANDING A TANGLED MESS

It's impossible to predict the future of Customer Jobs theory; however, one thing is for sure: a lot of people are confused. Moreover, there's little reason to think that will change in the future. Two reasons are:

Misattributions. One challenge with advancing Customer Jobs theory, is how many people repeat what others have written or said without investigating sources. For example, Alex Osterwalder wrote (2014):

> The jobs to be done concept was developed independently by several business thinkers including Anthony Ulwick of the consulting firm Strategyn, consultants Rick Pedi and Bob Moesta, and Professor Denise Nitterhouse of DePaul University. It was popularized by Clay Christensen and his consulting firm Innosight and Anthony Ulwick's Strategyn.

Here Osterwalder is trying to give due credit, but accidentally adds to the confusion:

> The citation makes it seem like Christensen, Nitterhouse, Moesta, Ulwick, and Pedi are talking about the same thing—while they are discussing wildly different things
>
> Christensen (2017) writes that Pedi and Moesta (not Ulwick and Nitterhouse) were the originators of Customer Jobs thinking
>
> While Denise Nitterhouse was cited as a co-author of the article "Finding the Right Job For Your Product" (Christensen et al

2007), she's a proponent of Customer Case Research (Berstell, Nitterhouse 1997) which isn't about JTBD. Moreover, a comment by "Denise Nitterhouse" claims that Nitterhouse is mistakenly attributed with the milkshake story (see article by Derek Christensen).

Repeating nascent, or passing, ideas as if they are well researched. Here's another challenge facing the future of JTBD: ideas are repeated without any proof or investigation of it's sources. For example, the idea that there are functional, social, and emotional jobs originates from just one line (Christensen 2003):

> The functional, emotional, and social dimensions of the jobs that customers need to get done constitute the circumstances in which they buy.

That's it! Just one line. No evidence, citation, or further clarification is given.

Over the years, many people have repeated and expanded upon this ontology of Jobs…but there's no experimental data or theoretical basis to support it. It's a textbook example of Argumentum ad Populum (i.e. "If many believe so, it is so").

THE FUTURE? USE WHAT'S HELPFUL. DON'T ASSUME ANYTHING

If you choose to get deeper into JTBD, know that it is quite the rabbit hole—for better or worse. My advice is to remain pragmatic, use what you feel is helpful, and be skeptical of what other people write and talk about.

The ultimate goal is to be great at making products that people will buy. The rest is just a means to that end.

REFERENCES

Bacharach, S. B. (1989). Organizational theories: Some criteria for evaluation. Academy of management review, 14(4), 496–515.

Bandura, A. (1997). Self-efficacy: The exercise of control. Macmillan.

Berstell, G., & Nitterhouse, D. (1997). Looking 'Outside the box'. Marketing Research, 9(2), 4

Bhattacherjee, A. (2012). Social science research: Principles, methods, and practices.

Carver, C. S., & Scheier, M. F. (2001). On the self-regulation of behavior. Cambridge University Press.

Chatterjee, S. (1998). Delivering desired outcomes efficiently: the creative key to competitive strategy. California Management Review, 40(2), 78–95.

Christou, G. & Saraiva, C. (2012). Hierarchical Task Analysis

Clayton, M. C., & Raynor, M. E. (2003). The Innovator's Solution: Creating and Sustaining Successful Growth. Harvard Business School Press: Boston, Massachusetts.

Christensen, C. M., Dillon, K., Hall, T., & Duncan, D. S. (2016). Competing against luck: The story of innovation and customer choice. Harper Business.

Christensen, C. M., Anthony, S. D., Berstell, G., & Nitterhouse, D. (2007). Finding the right job for your product. MIT Sloan Management Review, 48(3), 38.

Christensen, Derek, HIRING MILKSHAKES (AND OTHER SECRETS TO PRODUCT DEVELOPMENT).

Colquitt, J. A., & Zapata-Phelan, C. P. (2007). Trends in Theory Building and Theory Testing: A Five-Decade Study of the" Academy of Management Journal". The Academy of Management Journal, 1281–1303.

Deming, W. E. (2000). The new economics: for industry, government, education. MIT press.

Fried, J The Why before the Why.

Gibson, J. J. (2014). The ecological approach to visual perception: classic edition. Psychology Press.

Hackos, J. T., & Redish, J. (1998). User and task analysis for interface design.

Hassenzahl, M. (2010). Experience design: Technology for all the right reasons. Synthesis Lectures on Human-Centered Informatics, 3(1), 1–95.

Hornsby, P. (2010) Hierarchical Task Analysis

Klein, G. A. (2017). Sources of power: How people make decisions. MIT press.

Klement, A. (2016). When Coffee and Kale Compete.

Komninos "How to improve your UX designs with Task Analysis"

Levitt, T. (1983). Marketing Imagination: New. Simon and Schuster.

Norman, D. (1988). The Design of Everyday Things (Originally published: The psychology of everyday things). The Design of Everyday Things (Originally published: The psychology of everyday things).

Newell, A., & Simon, H. A. (1972). Human problem solving (Vol. 104, №9). Englewood Cliffs, NJ: Prentice-Hall.

Osterwalder, A., Pigneur, Y., Bernarda, G., & Smith, A. (2014). Value proposition design: How to create products and services customers want. John Wiley & Sons.

Powers, W. T. (1973). Behavior: The control of perception (p. ix). Chicago: Aldine.

Powers, W. T. (1973). Feedback: beyond behaviorism. Science, 179(4071), 351–356.

Simon, H. A. (1996). The sciences of the artificial. MIT press. Chicago

Spiek & Moesta 2014 Jobs to be Done Handbook

Saraiva, C. & Bevan, N. (2012). Cognitive Task Analysis

Ulwick, A. W. (2005). What customers want: Using outcome-driven innovation to create breakthrough products and services. McGraw-Hill Companies.

Ulwick, A. W., & Osterwalder, A. (2016). Jobs to be done: theory to practice.

Wiener, N. (1961). Cybernetics or Control and Communication in the Animal and the Machine (Vol. 25). MIT press.

17 Appendix: A Summary of Customer Jobs

What Is Customer Jobs (The Theory)?

A Job to be Done is a process: it starts, it runs, and it ends. The key difference, however, is that a JTBD describes how a customer changes or wishes to change. With this in mind, we define a JTBD as follows:

> A Job to be Done is the process a consumer goes through whenever she aims to transform her existing life-situation into a preferred one but cannot because there are constraints that stop her.

What Isn't A Customer Job?

If you are in doubt whether someone is describing a customer's JTBD, ask these questions:

> Does this describe an action?

> Can I visualize someone doing this?

If you answer "yes" to these questions, you're probably describing a solution for a JTBD and not a JTBD itself. Remember, a JTBD is not a task, activity, or has any functional characteristic. It describes a customer's desire to improve him-/herself—something that can neither be seen nor can be described in terms of actions or functional qualities.

What About Different Types of Jobs?

It is best to avoid coming up with different types of Jobs or stratifying them. Any attempt to do so will lead to logical inconsistencies and overlaps. It's best to keep it simple: each Job is a combination of various emotional forces.

What Are JTBD Principles?

Customers don't want your product or what it does; they want help making their lives better (i.e., they want progress).

People have Jobs; things don't.

Competition is defined in the minds of customers, and they use progress as their criterion.

When customers start using a solution for a JTBD, they stop using something else.

Innovation opportunities exist when customers exhibit compensatory behaviors.

Favor progress over outcomes and goals.

Progress defines value; contrast reveals value.

Solutions for Jobs deliver value beyond the moment of use.

Producers, consumers, solutions, and Jobs should be thought of as parts of a system that work together to evolve markets.

18 Appendix: Summary of Putting Customer Jobs to Work

Chapter 4

Ask customers about what they've done, not just what they want. Confirm it if you can.

Ask the right questions to learn how your customers view competition.

Learn what kind of progress customers are seeking. What's their emotional motivation (JTBD)? Use that to segment competition.

Ask yourself, "From which budget will my product take away money?"

Create better marketing material by speaking to your customers' JTBD.

Focus on delivering emotional progress (getting a Job Done). Don't focus solely on functionality.

Chapter 5

How do you convince teammates or management to change a product? Frame design challenges as a JTBD.

Dig deeper when you tap into a struggle or aspiration. How have customers tried to solve it before?

Determine if anxiety is a competitor. If it is, find ways of reducing it.

Be suspicious of the "impulse purchase" concept. No purchase is random.

Chapter 6

Don't depend on demographics.

Create better advertising and promotional material by speaking to what customers value.

Teams become more motivated, build consensus, and share a vision when they do JTBD research together.

Chapter 7

First, study the push and pull.

Dig into inertia and anxiety after identifying push and pull.

Fight anxiety and generate pull by helping customers visualize the progress they will make by using your product.

Reduce anxiety-in-choice with trials, refunds, and discounts.

Identify any habits-in-use that keep customers from using your product. Adjust your product to help them along.

Chapter 8

Create a constancy of purpose to innovate for your organization.

Discover the customers' JTBD by focusing on what doesn't change.

Before you make anything, have a clear picture in your mind of what customers will stop doing.

Chapter 9

Don't restrict competition to products with similar functionality or physical characteristics.

Talk with your customers!

Confirm that competition exists between products by finding customers who switched.

Do you think you're creating a new market? Think again.

Know what budget you're taking away from.

Continually refresh the competitive landscape with ongoing feedback from customers.

Remember that not every JTBD needs to be solved with a product that customers buy.

Chapter 10

Begin by identifying a struggle or aspiration. Start wide and get progressively narrow.

Find innovation opportunities when customers exhibit compensatory behaviors.

Chapter 11

Innovation opportunities are found through looking for specific data.

Know the difference between a struggling customer and a merely inconvenienced customer.

Great advertising comes from speaking to the customers' struggling moment.

Digging deep into customer motivation reveals innovation opportunities.

You can deliver progress to your customers' JTBD by offering a set of products that work together as a system.

Chapter 12

Grow your business, reduce churn, and capture more profits by delivering progress to customers.

Unlock your innovation creativity by asking, "What comes after?"

Chapter 13

Grow your business by unlocking new aspirations and offering products for them.

Think of your business as delivering a combination of products that work together to forward the system of progress.

Find product opportunities by looking forward and backward on the system of progress.

Chapter 14

Persuade customers to reject their current products by changing their JTBD.

Bring focus to which system of progress you're solving for by splitting up products that deliver different types of progress.

19 NOTES

[1] From Joseph Schumpeter's book Capitalism, Socialism, and Democracy, https://goo.gl/k3EG5d. Chart data are from Richard Foster's analysis, http://goo.gl/KngXcR.

[2] The story of Kodak's management rejecting digital camera from an article in the New York Times by James Estrin, http://goo.gl/mZMMOL.

[3] Sunk-cost fallacy from Hal R. Arkes and Catherine Blumer's The Psychology of Sunk Cost, https://goo.gl/fZ4JmL. Sunk-cost fallacy from Hal R. Arkes and Peter Ayton in The Sunk Cost and Concorde Effects: Are Humans Less Rational Than Lower Animals?, https://goo.gl/4EAHgF.

[4] Donald Norman's Human-Centered Design Considered Harmful, https://goo.gl/gxy166.

[5] The Story of the Pony Express by G. D. Bradley, https://goo.gl/Owz7gy.

[6] Nocera, Joe. "The Inside History of the 'New Coke' Debacle." Bloomberg.com, Bloomberg, 3 Nov. 2017, www.bloomberg.com/view/articles/2017-11-03/the-inside-history-of-the-new-coke-debacle.

[7] Twitter's revenue via Marketwatch, https://goo.gl/S7IUtc.

[8] Quotes are from George Box, https://goo.gl/vhxFTc; Deming and Lyon Nelson, https://goo.gl/08h0Wp; and Ronald H. Coase, https://goo.gl/744P5H.

[9] Deming's 1st, 2nd, and 5th Deadly Diseases, https://goo.gl/J4mvvQ.

[10] Steve Blank's article, "No Business Plan Survives First Contact with a Customer—The 5.2 Billion Dollar Mistake," http://goo.gl/tdlWio.

[11] Freud, S. (2005). Civilization and its discontents. WW Norton & Company.

[12] Charles Revson's quote, http://goo.gl/SjjWYt.

[13] 2016 Letter to Shareholders, https://blog.aboutamazon.com/working-at-amazon/2016-letter-to-shareholders

[14] Norman, D. (2013). The design of everyday things: Revised and expanded edition. Basic Books (AZ).

[15] Deming's quotes that appear in this section come from Deming's Quality, Productivity, and Competitive Position, https://goo.gl/a3CIzm and Out of the Crisis, https://goo.gl/3xgH8t.

[16] Revlon's revenue from Yahoo finance, http://goo.gl/7p5RS9.

[17] The "customers want a quarter inch hole" comes from Leo McGinneva, https://goo.gl/EM761j.

[18] Baking soda time line, http://goo.gl/p3bVK3.

[19] Segway for tour groups and police, http://goo.gl/C8ulJ1.

[20] Thanks to Bob Moesta for the pizza vs. steak example.

[21] Look for "WYSIATI". Kahneman, D. (2011). Thinking, fast and slow. Macmillan.

[22] Learn about revealed preference vs. stated preference from Paul Samuelson's "A Note on the Pure Theory of Consumer's Behavior," Economica, 1938. H. S. Houthakker's "Revealed Preference and the Utility Function," Economica, 1950. M. K. Richter's "Revealed Preference Theory," Econometrica: Journal of the Econometric Society, 1966.

[23] Preference reversal is explained in The Causes of Preference Reversal by Amos Tversky, Paul Slovic, and Daniel Kahneman, https://goo.gl/uv88iz.

[24] Read about expectations being violated in Gary Klein's Sources of Power: How People Make Decisions, https://goo.gl/LVvRkf.

[25] Elon Musk in *The Secret Tesla Motors Master Plan (Just between You and Me)*, http://goo.gl/A99Iq and *Master Plan, Part Deux*, http://goo.gl/d7KGCv. Tesla preorders from Tom Warren's Tesla Has Received Almost 400,000 Preorders for the Model 3, http://goo.gl/CM2Hw7.

[26] The "runaway best-seller" quote is from Harvard Business School's Tata Nano—The People's Car by faculty K. Palepu, B. N. Anand, and R. Tahilyani, https://goo.gl/xYlnBB. Clayton Christensen describes the Nano's disruptive potential in his book The Innovator's DNA, https://goo.gl/PQod00.

[27] Facts and figures about the Nano's flop (1) Indian Express "Sales of Tata Nano, World's Cheapest Car, Set to Hit Six-Year Lows," http://goo.gl/6hgd3O; (2) Wall Street Journal, "Why the World's Cheapest Car Flopped," http://goo.gl/Fq2eJT; (3)

Hindu Business Line, "Tata Motors' Nano Sales Continue to Dwindle," http://goo.gl/NXKEiF; (4) Business Insider, "This Is Why the Cheapest Car in the World Is a Huge Failure," http://goo.gl/yMUXnN; (5) Firstpost, "Bill Gates' Favorite Business Book Tells Us Why Tata Nano 'Really' Failed," http://goo.gl/89NVcd.

[28] "Tata Nano Crash during Handling Test—Not Really a Stable Car," http://goo.gl/sW0CRP and "Where Did It All Go Wrong for Tata's Nano?" http://goo.gl/Ekp6N9.

[29] "Tata GenX Nano Launched" by Vikas Yogi, http://goo.gl/RVUjVN.

[30] George Loewenstein describes anticipatory emotions and anticipated emotions in Risk as Feelings, https://goo.gl/KXZttM.

[31] Gary Klein NDM and mental simulation from Sources of Power, https://goo.gl/TkfSjV.

[32] How the chotuKool started from Innosight's Innovation Case Study, http://goo.gl/IeZwXL. Also see "Godrej Chotukool: A Cooling Solution for Mass Markets" by C. Dhanraj, B. Suram, and P. Vemuri from Harvard Business Review, https://goo.gl/HfnKRs.

[33] George Meneze's quote about selling millions of chotuKools from Fundamentals of Management: Asia Pacific Edition, https://goo.gl/z14cWj. chotuKool wins Edison Award from Innosight, http://goo.gl/hF3IXh and http://goo.gl/wpfvGn. Dr. Christensen praising the chotuKool, http://goo.gl/ioRFAK. Harvard Business School praising the chotuKool "Godrej Chotukool: A Cooling Solution for Mass Markets," http://goo.gl/75UmXn. Harvard Business School case study "Little Cool, Big Opportunity" by Rory McDonald, Derek van Bever, and Efosa Ojomo, https://goo.gl/W0niu3. Reference to water purifier and chotuWash "At Godrej, ChotuKool Spawns Major Business Strategy," http://goo.gl/hLK5l1 and "Multinational Companies Are Becoming Indian: Godrej's George Menezes," http://goo.gl/MgygOr. More on the chotuWash, http://goo.gl/S57eu9 and "A Small Innovation Leads to the Next Big Thing," http://goo.gl/BGB226.

[34] Only fifteen thousand chotuKools from S. Sharma's article in DNA India, "At Godrej, ChotuKool Spawns Major Business Strategy," http://goo.gl/4oxFQ1. Also in Engineering Applications in Sustainable Design and Development by Bradley Striebig, Adebayo A. Ogundipe, and Maria Papadakis (Nelson Education, 2015), p. 664. The chotuKool was first released in the state of Maharashtra: population 114.2 million. In "Back to Business Fundamentals: Making "Bottom of the Pyramid" Relevant to Core Business," E. Simanis, M. Milstein, and D. Ménascé point out that the chotuKool was celebrated by Godrej before any units were sold, https://goo.gl/gfFiL3. Comments about the chotuKool's failure, as well as the general flaw with disruptive innovations

are echoed here: P. Soni (2014), "Why Corporate Frugal Innovations Fail and Grassroots Frugal Innovations Succeed," http://goo.gl/rqcX0w.

[35] Navroze Godrej's comment, "Today it is a lifestyle product that people use in cars," is from K. Vijayraghavan's article from the Economic Times, "Godrej & Boyce Is Getting Sexier, in a Hurry," http://goo.gl/fBhZA0. G. Sunderraman's comment, "We are now targeting a midlevel buyer," appeared in the article, "Godrej's chotuKool Fridges to Flaunt Heritage Art Designs by Amrita Nair-Ghaswalla," http://goo.gl/wgosLI. G. Sunderraman's comment, "How can you expect poor consumers with a minimum sustenance to be your pot of gold?" appeared in K. Vijayraghavan's article, "Companies Like Nokia, Philips, HUL, Godrej Eye Emerging Middle Class," Economic Times, http://goo.gl/y8vWXW.

[36] These quotes and alternative solutions are mentioned in the case study previously referenced, "Godrej Chotukool: A Cooling Solution for Mass Markets," https://goo.gl/HfnKRs. The MittiCool as an alternative to the chotuKool is mentioned by P. Soni, "Why Corporate Frugal Innovations Fail and Grassroots Frugal Innovations Succeed," http://goo.gl/jvZIyu.

[37] Navroze Godrej's quote comes from Innosight's case study showcasing the chotuKool, http://goo.gl/4426vO.

[38] Stories like this are repeated in books like Christensen's The Innovator's Dilemma, https://goo.gl/hQVOvm. See also Christensen's (1) Harvard Business Review article, "What Is Disruptive Innovation?" https://goo.gl/jvoqKB; (2) his personal home page, Disruptive Innovation "Key Concepts," https://goo.gl/0APjIE; (3) from the Christensen Institute Disruptive Innovation, https://goo.gl/KkEVm1. It's also echoed in Jill Lepore's article, "What the Gospel of Innovation Gets Wrong," https://goo.gl/KQyJ6x. Here's a good video of Christensen selling this mainframe theory at the Saïd Business School, http://goo.gl/p9TCti.

[39] Sacconaghi's quote can be found in the Economist article, "Old Dog, New Tricks," http://goo.gl/atcnj1.

[40] Numbers on mainframe install base from a white paper by Janet L. Sun titled, "Don't Believe the Myth—Information about the Mainframe," https://goo.gl/cdfqcz.

[41] Women as "computers" from J. Gumbrecht's article, "Rediscovering WWII's Female 'Computers,'" http://goo.gl/Xk77Ni. R. Eveleth wrote "Computer Programming Used to Be Women's Work," http://goo.gl/ML4XWL. L. Sydell wrote "The Forgotten Female Programmers Who Created Modern Tech," http://goo.gl/GWfyYb. More information about the Friden, http://goo.gl/GdpeUu. Another example of this workflow is from B. Evans's article, "Office, Messaging and Verbs," http://goo.gl/AN4alF.

[42] Companies that use mainframes today are recorded by C. Saran, "Is the Time Right for a Mainframe Renaissance?" http://goo.gl/9QmNrs.

[43] These are quotes from an interview with Dr. Nrom in PC Magazine from 1984, https://goo.gl/esl6FC.

[44] IBM 5100 commercial, http://goo.gl/IjoHiH. Commodore Vic-20 commercial, http://goo.gl/nWxkCL. Apple IIe commercials, http://goo.gl/Dbjz0q and http://goo.gl/9WEO4Y. Tandy 1000 commercials, http://goo.gl/Wqaf0Y and http://goo.gl/JbIapW.

[45] Kim S. Nash wrote "Johnson & Johnson Targets 85% of Apps in Cloud by 2018," http://goo.gl/a8mCBb.

[46] A summary of the data for this chart can be found on The Motley Fool article, "Don't Worry about IBM's Mainframe Sales Collapse," http://goo.gl/crfFj8. A good summary of the current state of mainframe sales and IBM's revenue from them, "IBM Reports 2Q2014 Earnings: Mainframe Business Humming," http://goo.gl/1g87q2. IBM's 2014 annual report, http://goo.gl/vnmegN.report, http://goo.gl/vnmegN.

Data on PC margins are found here in Z. Epstein's article, "You Won't Believe How Little Windows PC Makers Earn for Each PC Sold," http://goo.gl/4GbPlL. Sad state of PC from Zacks PC, "Market Plight Continues in Q3 Say Gartner, IDC," http://goo.gl/zWWv9m. Mainframes keeping up with needs of technology is discussed in Steve Lohr's article, "IBM Mainframe Evolves to Serve the Digital World," http://goo.gl/xTPglX. See also Don Clark's Wall Street Journal article, "IBM Moves to Refresh Mainframe Line," http://goo.gl/Wue5S2.

[47] Books referenced: (1) Frederick Winslow Taylor, The Principles of Scientific Management, https://goo.gl/4gAie9; (2) Robert H. Waterman and Tom Peter, In Search of Excellence, https://goo.gl/q3liSH; (3) James Charles Collins and Jerry I. Porras, Built to Last, https://goo.gl/FPVFBU; (4) James Charles Collins, Good to Great, https://goo.gl/LBnuo0; (5) Clayton Christensen, The Innovator's Dilemma, https://goo.gl/AhHjEo.

[48] Works referenced: (1) Phil Rosenzweig, The Halo Effect, https://goo.gl/rjAOju; (2) Daniel Kahneman, Thinking, Fast and Slow, https://goo.gl/ExXDSb; (3) Feynman's Caltech commencement address given in 1974, https://goo.gl/uZDqLJ. "Fooled by Randomness" is adapted from Nassim Nicholas Taleb's books Fooled by Randomness, https://goo.gl/XNoOgA, and The Black Swan, https://goo.gl/20f63l

[49] See Robert McMillan's Wall Street Journal article, "PC Sales Drop to Historic Lows," http://goo.gl/ls3TvR.

⁵⁰ Des Traynor's quote comes from "Not All Good Products Make Good Businesses," http://goo.gl/ERsmHM.

⁵¹ Read about Deming and Ford, http://goo.gl/khzdpt and http://goo.gl/sS4WJa.

⁵² Read about DDT and its effect on the ecosystem at http://goo.gl/KZCeDu.

⁵³ This is another example of Gary Klein's mental simulation, https://goo.gl/0GjEji.

⁵⁴ Shewhart Cycle: Walter Andrew Shewhart, Economic Control of Quality of Manufactured Product (ASQ Quality Press, 1931). Walter Andrew Shewhart and William Edwards Deming, Statistical Method from the Viewpoint of Quality Control (Courier Corporation, 1939). More history of the Shewhart Cycle and PDSA from Ronald Moen's Foundation and History of the PDSA Cycle, http://goo.gl/cm6fNN.

⁵⁵ Apple's iPhone numbers from statista, http://goo.gl/5TiRmr. Applications in App Store, http://goo.gl/wqL8Lm. Service vs. system: Instead of calling a collection of products a service, you could call them a system—a smaller system that contributes to the larger system of progress. Use whatever language is most comfortable for you.

⁵⁶ Read Tim Cook's statement during an earnings report by R. Ritchie, "This Is Tim: Apple's CEO on the Company's 2016 Q3 Earnings," http://goo.gl/ujQtqX.

⁵⁷ Special thanks to David Wu for this example: "If They Don't Ask about the Price It's Absolute Bunk," http://goo.gl/Nyzr8N. Spirit Airlines financials, http://goo.gl/ZexDI2. Read about customer complaints about Spirit Airlines in Bloomberg article, "The Most Hated US Airline Is Also the Most Profitable," http://goo.gl/9qGpmr.

⁵⁸ Ryanair's financials, http://goo.gl/BrQosV. Ryanair brand ranking, http://goo.gl/tRPwhw.

⁵⁹ Steve Ballmer's comments on the iPhone, http://goo.gl/7Eqjo8.

⁶⁰ Microsoft's numbers, "Windows Phone Market Share Sinks Below 1 Percent," by T. Warren, http://goo.gl/CHxi8b.

⁶¹ Steve Jobs and empathy: A Monk without Empathy, by K. C. Ifeanyi, http://goo.gl/WVAoi6. Steve Jobs quotes: (1) Owen Linzmayer, "Steve Jobs' Best Quotes Ever," http://goo.gl/as6xj3Holtzclaw; (2) Eric Holtzclaw, "The 1 Basic Question That Leads to Product Innovation," http://goo.gl/69kHMU.

[62] Deming's quote from an interview titled, "Management Today Does Not Know What Its Job Is" (part 1), http://goo.gl/efM4qf.

[63] "Context-Dependent Preferences," by Amos Tversky and Itamar Simonson, https://goo.gl/MK4Hfv. Learn about trade-off contrast and extremeness aversion in Amos Tversky and Itamar Simonson, "Choice in Context: Tradeoff Contrast and Extremeness Aversion," https://goo.gl/btJAh8. Learn about preference reversals: (1) Amos Tversky and Richard H. Thaler, "Anomalies: Preference Reversals," https://goo.gl/Po5sCJ; (2) A. Tversky, P. Slovic, and D. Kahneman, "The Causes of Preference Reversal," https://goo.gl/23A0sc. Learn about intransitivity of preference: Amos Tversky, "Intransitivity of Preferences," https://goo.gl/6r9K0X.

[64] Deming's quote from an interview, "Management Today Does Not Know What Its Job Is" (part 1), http://goo.gl/glVo4i. Steve Jobs quotes, http://goo.gl/z2yaUw.

[65] Read more about Joanna's story, http://goo.gl/xG7xcE.

[66] Read about the flaw here: http://fortune.com/2016/08/08/qualcomm-android-quadrooter/

[67] "Indians Spurn Snacks, Shampoo to Load Their Smartphones", https://www.wsj.com/articles/indians-spurn-snacks-shampoo-to-load-their-smartphones-1471163223

Made in the USA
Columbia, SC
13 May 2019